A crazy story about re-
learning life lessons in
Alaska's deadly wilderness

...What could go wrong?

I0093291

NO
NEW
LESSONS

PAUL R. WHITE

W

W

White House Ops

No New Lessons
Paul R. White
Published by White House Ops
Imprint by 1of5project.com
www.1of5project.com
whitehouseops@gmail.com

The 1 of 5 Project teaches better decision-making, mental discipline, and physical well-being to improve your own standard. We help guide how to plan, execute, and debrief any goal. The 1 of 5 Project helps people silence the quitter inside, gives them tools to win, and leads them to be champions in the game of life.

SpringboardBooks

This book was created in collaboration with Springboard Books.

Springboard Books guides authors and writers in all the stages of book creation, including editing, cover design, formatting, and marketing. Springboard Books helps aspiring authors and businesses write and publish high-quality books they can use as powerful marketing tools to stand out from the competition and get more sales. Learn more at www.springboardbookpros.com

Book design by Steve Plummer, www.spbookdesign.com
Paperback: 979-8-9870020-0-1 eBook: 979-8-9870020-1-8

DO YOU WANT TO BE A CHAMPION?
DO YOU WANT TO LEARN HOW TO CONSISTENTLY WIN AT LIFE?

Visit https://1of5project.com to learn what it takes to win in every area of your life.

The 1 of 5 Project's Mission Statement:

IMPROVE. IGNITE. INSPIRE.

The 1 of 5 Project's mission is to Improve your personal standard, Ignite change with a champion's mindset, and Inspire others through your own actions.

https://1of5project.com

Regardless of your starting point, *The 1 of 5* Project will guide you to better decision-making, mental discipline, and physical well-being to improve your own standard and increase everyone's average.

The 1 of 5 Project applies proven techniques from intense experiences as a championship winning coach and combat aviation veteran to serve clients with problem solving, goal setting, planning and performance. Start with yourself. Change the world.

At *The 1 of 5*, we specialize in providing life coaching services via books, coaching, public speaking engagements, emails and more.

Visit https://1of5project.com to learn more.

Dedicated to those with an adventurous
spirit and have the guts to go for it.

Roscoe, Banzai, Smokus (left to right.) Behind us is the
bus where Chris McCandless died in 1992.

So there I was. In June 2009, two of my friends and I hiked down the Stampede Trail near Healy, Alaska in search of a bus in the wilderness. Adhering to a strict timeline and with minimal gear, we survived off determination, bad decisions and maybe even some magic. Perpetually cold, wet and hungry, we re-learned about the pursuit of happiness and humor in the Alaskan bush.

—ROSCOE

We shall not cease from exploration, and the end of all our exploring will be to arrive where we started and know the place for the first time.

—T. S. ELIOT

If one advances confidently in the direction of his dreams, and endeavors to live the life, which he has imagined, he will meet with a success unexpected in common hours. He will put some things behind, will pass an invisible boundary; new, universal, and more liberal laws will begin to establish themselves around and within him; or the old laws be expanded, and interpreted in his favor in a more liberal sense, and he will live with the license of a higher order of beings.

—HENRY DAVID THOREAU

There is a place called adventure that lives just on the horizon. It calls us forth, over the next ridge and around the next bend. It's where life's good stories live, the ones that will be told around campfires for a lifetime and more. But adventure doesn't give up her secrets easily. She keeps them hidden from all but the most willing. Willing to pay the asking price.

—CLAY HAYES, "ALONE" SEASON 8 WINNER

Happiness is only real when shared.

—CHRIS MCCANDLESS

NO NEW LESSONS

PROLOGUE

THIS IS NOT a Chris McCandless biography or memoir by any stretch. If anyone reads this with the idea they will somehow learn the secret to what drove a young man into the wilderness where he ultimately met his demise, they will be extremely disappointed. I am not emotional one way or another about any ideal or mentality surrounding the mystery of Chris McCandless.

The following story is simply about a weekend hiking trip between three friends and the ridiculous path we took to get to a bus in the woods. The bus was only a destination. It could have very well been a lake, summit of a mountain, watchtower, or a pub downtown. The bus provided motivation to complete something we started and gave us a reason to keep walking farther. That is all. We did not have a significant emotional event as we approached our destination. In fact, Banzai's video immediately following an uneventful arrival at the bus is explicitly void of emotion as he states with as much flat melancholy in as monotone speech as he could muster, "Ok, here we are, it's a bus, woohoo." He could not have added less inflection, surprise, or emphasis.

Many, many people are captivated by the "Chris McCandless Experience" and are driven to the bus like it's a holy place or shrine. In sharp contrast, locals near the area have varying degrees of distain toward the bus. They argue Chris got what he earned due to his lack of preparedness, and anyone who attempts to reach the bus is silly, foolhardy and should expect the same.

Additionally, local authorities rescued many hikers every year attempting to reach the bus, most of which are grossly mis outfitted for the long hike. Just a few years ago, the State Troopers rescued two young men who had gone missing for a few days. When the Troopers found them, they had no water or food, were dressed in shorts and had plastic bags covering their sneakers. Accidents happen, sure, but this kind of stuff is one hundred percent preventable.

The memories we share are not of that tattered, beaten, broken down shell of a bus. We tell stories of the journey getting there and back, the people who impacted us along the way and the circumstances surrounding every decision. At no time over the past years have we sat and debated what makes the "Magic Bus" magic at all. We honestly didn't, and still don't care. It was just a domino to knock down, nothing more.

Preparing to write this down, finally after a decade of sitting on it, I re-read much of the literature and articles making that bus a famed destination. I watched hours of videos on YouTube and scanned through hundreds of photos on the Internet, as well as organizing and inspecting my own personal collection. The research took me right back to that trail, and I was able to relive the experience one word at a time.

Alaska is still wild. To treat her as any different is a mistake that can lead to failure.

PRE-BRIEFING

I'D LIKE TO acknowledge a few things up front to serve as my ultimate disclaimer for what follows. First, this is not an attempt at polished scholarship. I just wanted to tell a story like we were sitting around a campfire. What follows is my first-hand account of a great adventure with two friends created from memory, for memories.

I write like I talk, and I am no expert with the English language, by any stretch. Hopefully those who read this can imagine listening to me tell a story after a few beers rather than just reading it. An old friend of mine had a saying—WUSIWUG—What u see is what u get.

Second, for the naysayers who doubted our resolve: Thanks for the motivation. Proving you all wrong makes me feel warm and fuzzy inside, so thank you.

Lastly, and very selfishly, thanks to Banzai and Smokus for making this possible for me. Had you not been blissfully ignorant and compliant enough to follow along into the great unknown I would never have had this memory. Thanks. I write this for one reason and one reason only: so we three may have the memory engrained forever. One day, when we are old and senile, we can grab this off the shelf and have story time during our bridge game at the old folk's home. I hope you enjoy this journey as much as I've enjoyed jotting it down.

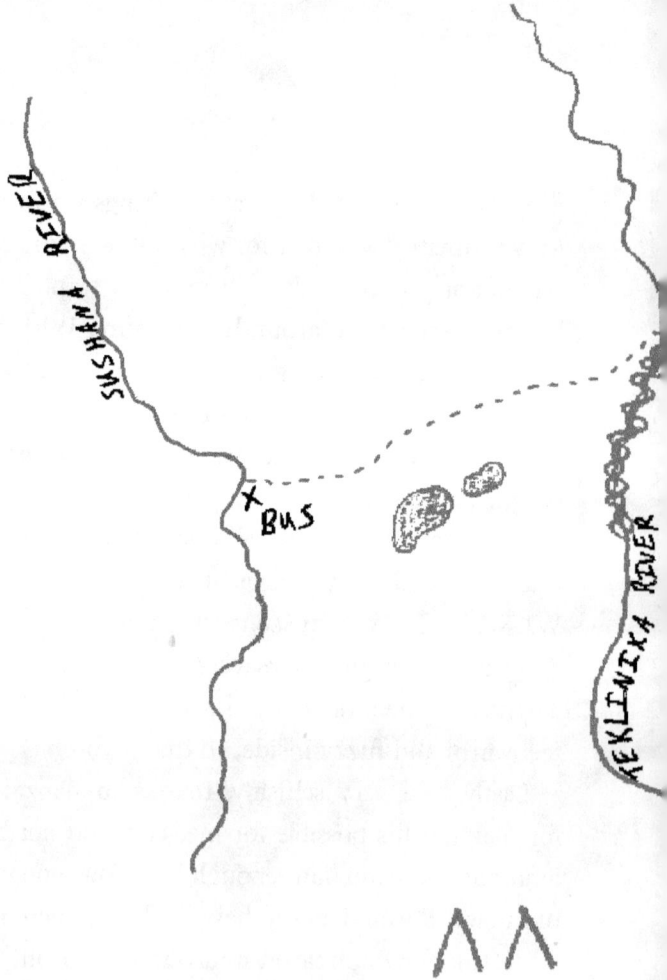

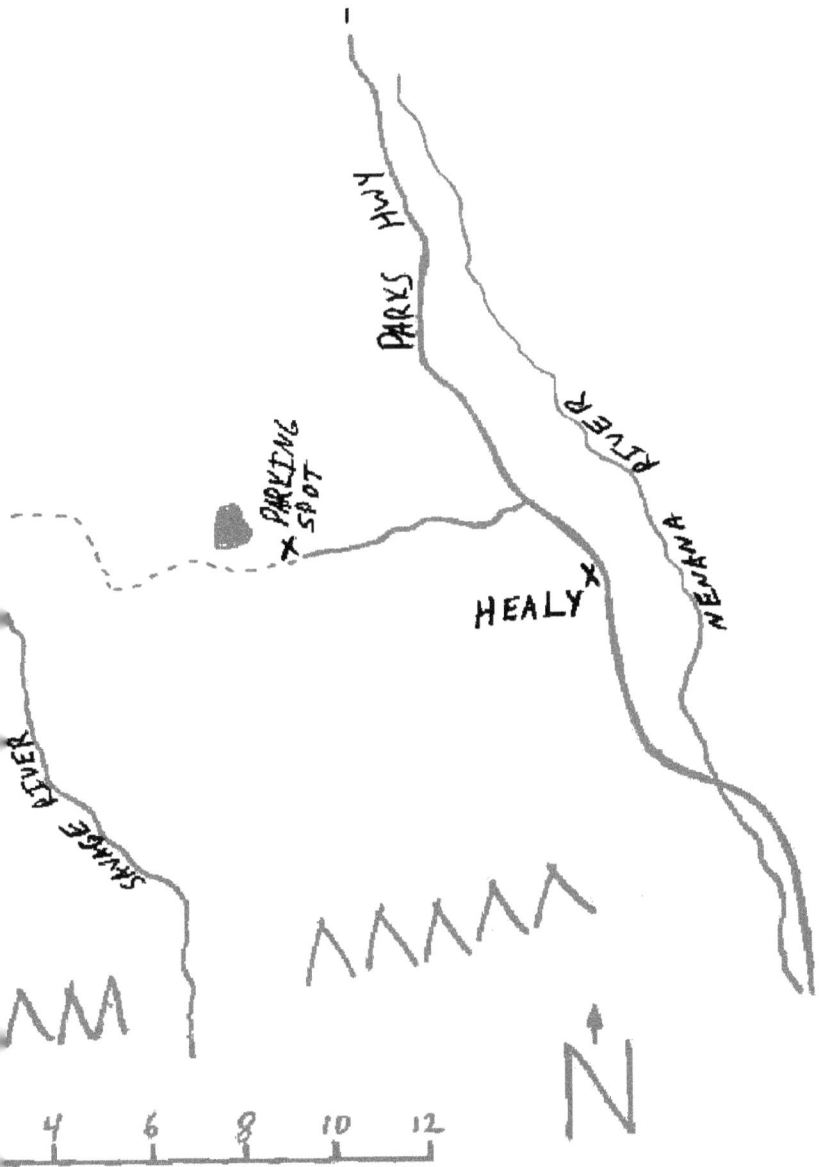

PARKS HWY

NENANA RIVER

PARKING SPOT

HEALY X

SAVAGE RIVER

N

4   6   8   10   12

THE END

"That was the best cheeseburger I've ever had!"

How many people can remember the best cheeseburger they have ever eaten? I'm not talking about a trip you took and had a good meal. It doesn't matter how much it cost. I'm talking about the BEST damn burger you've ever eaten—the one that had meaning, flavor, and emotion. The one that if you hadn't had that burger your life would somehow be different. The way the cheese fused with the patty to become a single entity. The lettuce exploring the border of what is considered just a layer of a burger versus being a complete side salad. The tomato that adds just the right amount of color, juice and flavor to compliment the mustard and mayo. How savory that burger was, but still not complete without the explosion and tart of the pickle that somehow added just the right amount of crunch.

This is not your Friday-night Sonic cheeseburger or the In-and-Out Animal style off the "secret" menu. This is not a super awesome, medium rare bacon cheeseburger from

Texas Roadhouse or some other chain restaurant. This isn't even a classy burger from some over-priced highfalutin joint I can't go into on account of the dress code. This burger was epic. This burger was life.

All that said, this burger was a simple, frozen, cheap-ass patty, fried on a griddle by what was likely an overweight, under paid fry cook with a beard. No, he probably didn't wear the beard net to cover his ridiculously homely face pubes. The burger was on the regular menu and cost no more than $10. The complimentary fries were nothing special, probably not even salted. So, what made this very basic, seemingly plain burger so wonderful that I would remember the exact date, time, place, and accompaniment? Trust me, it wasn't the burger. It was the preceding 30 or so hours leading up to that meal that cemented it in my memory forever. As I write this, it's more than 13 years later, and I still remember the details as if it happened yesterday.

Memory is a funny thing. As a military flight instructor, I have studied how to get information to "stick" in a person's mind to become knowledge. *Primacy* is the concept whereby those events learned first in a series are often the ones that stick the hardest. In other words, it's hard to teach an old dog, new tricks. Those things learned first often create a strong, almost unshakable impression. Bad habits learned early are hard to break. *Recency* is an axiom that is best described as the things experienced most recently are the best remembered. An individual remembers more clearly yesterday's events versus yester-years.' *Intensity* requires a vivid, dramatic, or exciting experience in order to teach above what routine or boring lessons can. *Intensity* creates an unbreakable memory in some cases. This concept is fundamental to understanding Post Traumatic Stress Disorder. Those events tied to an extraordinary event seem to resonate so loudly in a memory that they can impair future exercise in the same arena.

Intensity is the phenomenon that makes me remember that very plain, very simple cheeseburger. The succulent explosion of varying flavors was nothing but a biproduct of the events leading up to it. The true nature of the intensity was the lack of nourishment during what ended up being a battle of wills with three friends on an adventure that was grossly under planned and insidiously dangerous. The only thing I could think of at the time was I had not eaten in more than 20 hours, but I had hiked somewhere around 50 miles through cold, muddy, icy, glacial river runoff, peat bogs and mud. It felt like my stomach was eating itself. All I had was some oatmeal at around 1300 the day prior and some water purified from a river flowing with glacier silt. At this point in the trip, I had no thoughts except how to replace all the calories I had lost, my feet hurt like a son-of-a-bitch and I wanted to sleep forever.

I try to live my life by a few very simple rules.

- Focus forward and not backward. Control what you can control.

- Win the next play.

- Maintain a positive attitude, pay attention, and give maximum effort.

- Have a plan, have a backup plan, stick to the plan, and always have an exit strategy.

- Make the best decision you can with the information you have.

- Keep your eyes on the horizon and always improve your position.

As an aside, another good rule to live by is nothing good happens in Vegas after midnight.

Sometimes the cosmos aligns just perfectly, creating a decision point that impacts you and those around you. One such alignment occurred in June 2009. Struggling through our journey, we were presented with many decision points. Each time we chose a path we were getting closer to our goal. If we had made a different choice at any of those pivotal moments, we would have altered our trip such that we likely would not have made it.

What follows is a first-hand account of how a series of (arguably bad) decisions combined with influence on others led to an exciting, almost deadly, but ultimately enlightening and exhilarating hike through the Alaskan wilderness. At its core, it was just three friends on a hiking trip. Looking back, I think we each re-learned some good life lessons, found out a bit about ourselves, and we all certainly walked away with simultaneous feelings of "That was epic" and "I'm not doing that again".

Spoiler alert, you know how the story ends, but I hope the following journey of how we got there is as much fun as it was to be there. Beginning at the end: the cheeseburger. The journey that got us to that very plain, exceptionally epic burger was fun, scary, terrible, exciting, defeating, exhilarating, memorable, forgettable and unforgettable.

The best cheeseburger I ever had was in Healy, Alaska, just after 1000 on Sunday morning, June 21, 2009, but the story begins hours, days, weeks, maybe even months before.

ALASKA

RETIRED FROM THE United States Air Force in 2018, but in 2009 I was still on active duty when my squadron deployed to Eielson AFB, Alaska for Exercise NORTHERN EDGE 2009. We were scheduled to be in Alaska for three weeks in support of a joint exercise that rivals one of the Air Force's largest in both size and scope. Our weekends were mostly ours to do with as we pleased, and my goal was to spend as much time in the wilderness as possible enjoying everything Alaska had to offer in June.

The months leading up to the deployment were intense, but we always kept sight of the potential fun of being in Alaska in June. Early summer is arguably the best time of year to be in Alaska. Days are long, weather is usually good, rivers are flowing, and fish are running and biting. Alaska in June feels alive. Almost daily there was a meeting centered solely on what the evening fun would entail. More often than not, that fun included getting out into the Alaskan wilderness in some capacity. Whether hiking, fishing, camping or just going for a drive, we all wanted to maximize our time in one of the most stunning places on earth.

One of our fellow squadron members had been stationed at
Elmendorf AFB in Anchorage a few years earlier, so it made
sense for him to take the lead in planning a weekend expedition and group trip of some sort. After much deliberation
and inputs from others, he thought it would be a good idea to
get the entire squadron together for a salmon fishing trip on
the Copper River near Gulkana, Alaska. A great majority of
the folks going on the deployment had never been to Alaska
or fished for salmon before, so at first the idea sounded great
to everyone. The plan was for all of us to go out on a Friday
following a long week of flying, camp out next to the river,
drink whiskey and sing songs around a raging campfire, fish
a little, and generally just enjoy being out in nature with not
many rules. You know, man shit. A great way to wind down a
long week and relax a bit before doing it all again on Monday
(or Sunday afternoon).

Planning for the fishing trip was left for the one person in
charge to complete. The rest of the Squadron mates just sort of
trusted that he would do it right and we would end up having
a great time without having to do too much work. With the
planning phase nearing completion, we set up for a briefing
on what to expect. The initial brief on the fishing trip was
thorough and exciting. It seemed like the plan was going well
until he revealed the price. In the beginning when the idea
was pitched to the minions, the price was digestible at $100
per person. But it quickly rose to over $300 in just a few weeks.

Having lived in Alaska previously for over four years and
having caught every species of salmon in the state, I decided
that was a little too rich for my blood, so I bowed out grace-
fully. I've got mouths to feed and stuff. After socializing the

idea around with some of the others and venting my frustra-
tions, I learned at least two others shared my thoughts about
the price, so we got to work on a separate plan of our own.
We still wanted to experience all that nature stuff, but really
didn't care to spend $300 to sit in a boat and catch a fish with
a bunch of other dudes. Sorry, man-stew is not for me. For
those who have been salmon fishing, you know it's way more
involved than that, but whatever...

The single most limiting factor of how much we would be
able to do was how little time we would most likely be afforded.
We knew we had to be back to Eielson AFB no later than 1600
on Sunday. We also knew we had to use a rental, and we only
had a few assigned to our group. Most important, we knew
we would only have the gear we brought with us from home
in Idaho. With all these truths in mind, we narrowed our
adventure to just a few interesting destinations. We could stick
close to the base and just find a secluded place in the woods
to be isolated from the real world for a bit. We could go on the
fishing trip and just not fish, instead we would just enjoy the
brotherhood of the fighter squadron, cold evenings with warm
whiskey. Or, we could venture out a bit and see some of what
many consider America's most beautiful State.

Alaska, the 49th State, is a gem. I moved there in November
2000 from Panama City, Florida, and I can positively say
they were some of the best years of my life. My wife, son, and
I drove all the way in our Chevy Tahoe with little more than
a glorified magazine as a guide. My initial impressions of
Alaska were of grandeur and rugged wilderness. I marveled
at the raw, untouched, never-ending landscapes. I often told
people it was one of the rare places where you could drive

five minutes out of town, turn left and be lost in the wilderness. I've walked up on moose while hiking, met porcupines while four-wheeling, and I fished in a river opposite a brown bear trying to compete for the same fish. I have encountered mosquitoes so thick I had to wave my hand in front of my face as I walked, just to keep from ingesting them. I've been the coldest I've ever been in my life at minus 39.8 degrees Fahrenheit, and I've roasted in the Alaskan summer sun at a blistering 75 degrees. I've been so cold in my tent that I had my chocolate lab, Sarah Jane Rottendog, zipped in with me to cuddle for warmth. I've been hit in my car by a moose. I've seen the full spectrum of colors of the Aurora Borealis, or northern lights. I've stood next to glaciers and mountains that make a person feel tiny and insignificant. I've seen Mount McKinley and waded through peat bogs. I have witnessed a moose stand at a crosswalk at a four-way red-light intersection, wait on the little white dude flashy sign thingy that means cross, proceed across the street and start eating bushes in a bank parking lot, all in midday on a main street in downtown Anchorage.

Alaska offers a different perspective on what is important in life. These phenomena constantly remind me there are bigger things in this world than me—Internet, cell phones, Facebook, flashy cars. All those things are material and seemed insignificant when I got out to the middle of nowhere and just sat on a log and stared at the ripples in the water of a remote alpine lake. If a person cannot get their mind right there, then you probably need professional therapy.

Alaska is also host to Denali National Park. Becoming a national park in 1917, Denali National Park is larger than the entire state of New Jersey. The park consists largely of taiga tundra, wildlife, and of course the Alaska Range, home of Mount McKinley. At 20,310 feet in elevation, Mount McKinley is not only the highest peak in North America, but it ranks 3rd in the entire world in topographic prominence. Aside from the single, 92-mile road running along the north side of the range, the 6 million-acre Denali National Park is largely untouched by human hands. Again, Alaska can make a person feel insignificant in the grand scheme of life.

For many of the reasons listed above, we convinced ourselves that our best game plan was to go to Denali National Park and camp out "survival school" style (more on this later). The park was only a few hours' drive from Eielson AFB, which is just southeast of Fairbanks. Roads in the park for the most part were reported to be easy to travel, and the hiking trails were plentiful. This seemed to offer exactly what we were looking for. We wanted to get away from real life and enjoy God's country for a bit.

I thought I had it all planned out and figured we would be good to just "wing it" when we got there. The vision in my mind of simply parking in the parking lot, hiking out into the wilderness and hanging out for a couple days drinking whiskey by the fire literally made me lose sleep in anticipation of what was sure to be an epic adventure. My delusions were melted back into reality when I finally read up on the situation. I began to research the Park website only to find out how naïve my so-called "planning" had been. The single road in the park was only traveled by a private bus company. In other words, one cannot just drive up to the mountain, get out and go for it. Additionally, there were only a few approved campsites within reach. Finally, and worst of all, the rules clearly stated no open flames. No campfires. What a freaking buzzkill. More importantly, it presented another decision point. Do we stick to the plan? Go camping and fishing with the masses? Or come up with a completely new plan? We decided to open our aperture and look for something new and different. The decision to abandon the salmon fishing trip, then subsequently the Denali camping trip, was the first of many significant choices that would lead us down the path toward the Bus.

INCEPTION

I'M NOT NORMALLY one to blame others for my misfortune but let me just say this whole story is my wife's fault. My wife is a movie person. She loves the event of watching a film and figuring out what the authors, directors, or actors tried to convey through their performances. She enjoys the idea of determining her own interpretation of the story itself, but she hates the idea of not closing a film out. Those films that are open-ended and left to the viewers to decide the finish are frustrating for her. She needs closure. It was she who encouraged me to watch a movie called "Into the Wild", the 2007 film by Sean Penn, based on Jon Krakauer's book by the same name. I was skeptical at first because, as she knows, I am not like her with regard to films. I am much more of an instant gratification kind of guy. I like the shoot 'em ups. I like movies that are finite and don't leave me wondering what happened. That said, I do like adventure. I suppose I will always have a desire in me to see and do things I have never seen or done before. She tugged on that string until I caved, and we watched the movie.

This is not a review of the film, per se. But, spoiler alert,

I do have some thoughts. I walked away from the movie thinking it was a story about a spoiled rich kid who was trying to be rebellious, pushing himself too far beyond his personal capabilities, and ultimately paying the price with his own death. I realize this is an over-simplified explanation and arguably far from truth, but it was my initial impression. According to the movie, Chris McCandless left a life of ease and affluence for one as a nomadic wanderer, or "tramp" to use the slang vernacular. He transformed himself into a sort of nomadic vagabond, eventually re-naming himself Alexander Supertramp. His adventures and follies landed him in Alaska just beyond the northern boundary of Denali National Park outside Healy, Alaska. This is the portion of the movie that really grabbed my attention. The cinematic portrayal of Alaska dredged up memories and feelings of "Hey, I've been there." Though I had not been to his area or exact location, I had been to many places resembling the same topography, forest and tundra, trees and wildlife. That connection was the hook that kept me watching. Never mind the fact that I thought the entire movie was a lesson in all the wrong things to do when in the wilderness, the movie was somewhat entertaining, and I did enjoy it. Watching the movie led me to do some research on the story, which further led me to Jon Krakauer.

Krakauer is a writer formerly for Outside Magazine, an accomplished mountaineer, and the author of the 1996 book, "Into the Wild" among others. After skimming his article "Death of an Innocent", I decided to buy the book. The book, of course, is exponentially better than the movie in my opinion. Krakauer developed more depth to the characters and painted with great color the entire journey, particularly the Alaskan landscape. He also dug deeper into the how-and-why that would motivate a young man to take on such an adventure.

After a couple of years living on the road, McCandless ended up outside Healy, near Denali National Park. With all his possessions packed in a backpack, a small caliber rifle and a pair of borrowed rubber boots, Alex Supertramp set out in April 1992 toward the west, down the Stampede Trail just two miles north of Healy, crossed two rivers, and stumbled upon a broken-down Fairbanks city bus, in the wilderness. The bus had been there for years as part of a series of buses leading deep into the bush out to antimony mines. It had previously been retrofit with a mattress and a stove, so it made a perfect camp for a single person or small group. Situated on high ground near a running river, the Sushana, miners used the buses as stopovers on their journey in and out of the mines. As mining operations began to wane, the buses were all removed from the wilderness, all except the Sushana bus. That particular bus had broken an axel while being towed on the outgoing trip, so the mining company just left it where it sat, abandoned, for anyone to use in the future. McCandless homesteaded in the bus, enjoying the bounty of the surrounding wilderness. According to the book, McCandless lived in the bus well into summer, until he "found himself" and decided to return to civilization. He packed his things and headed east, but was blocked by the Teklanika River, which was running at peak intensity in July. He returned to his sanctuary at the bus, eventually meeting his demise just a few weeks later.

The abandoned Fairbanks city bus number 142 is now known to some as the "Magic Bus" based on how McCandless referred to it in his writings. A diary kept by McCandless describing his stay, was a major source for the book written by Krakauer and the 2007 movie, staring Emile Hirsch. Since McCandless' demise, but more so after the movie's release, many hikers have struggled with the rough Alaska conditions, attempting the pilgrimage to the bus, and several have died trying to reach the end. Hundreds have set out on the Stampede Trail heading for the wrecked bus. According to available data, there were at least 15 state search-and-rescue missions into the area from 2009 to 2017, retrieving either stranded, injured or otherwise imperiled travelers. As of this writing, there have been at least two deaths by drowning in the Teklinika River.

In December 2019 I randomly selected and was captivated by a "Joe Rogan Experience" podcast featuring Glenn Villeneuve. Glenn is an Alaskan bushman, most famous for his self-depicting role on the television reality show, "Life Below Zero." Listening to his testimony of how he got to where he is truly snared my curiosity and I hung on every word. From tales of getting chased by a pack of wolves, to eating the stomach contents of caribou, his description of living in the wilderness is nothing short of riveting.

One thing that really stood out to me and became more and more evident as Glenn told his story, was his level of planning, both the amount and the level of detail. He said he got the idea to live in the Brooks Range, 200 miles north of Fairbanks, while flying over the topographical divide of the Alaskan interior and the northern slope, years before. It took him seven years to plan it out and prepare to live off the land. When he finally made the plunge, he moved into a 100 square foot tent on a lake 60 miles from the nearest road and began his new life—living one with nature.

As of the date of that podcast, Glenn has lived there with his wife and kids for 17 years. He has battled through sickness and starvation, but always had some form of lifeline or exit strategy. He studied and learned how to fly and fix his float plane, kill, butcher, preserve and eat every part of an animal so nothing goes to waste, and build his own shelters. Glenn totally crushed it. McCandless did not.

The biggest mistake McCandless made, in my opinion, was he failed to really plan. For starters, he either had no concept of the time of year and the effects of the Alaskan winter or just completely disregarded both. April in Alaska is still very cold. The rivers, ponds and lakes he crossed in April were still partially frozen and not running at peak capacity, and the permafrost was frozen solid and covered with snow, making the route easily passable. The larger and more formidable of the two rivers on his path, the Teklanika River, is fed from a glacier of the same name high in the Denali Range. Though I do not know his exact circumstances because I wasn't there, it's easy to armchair quarterback the situation, knowing that in summer the river would swell and potentially become impassable.

McCandless also did not fully understand preserving meat for lengthy periods. As accounted in his diary, he shot and killed a moose with his rifle, and he was seemingly very proud of this accomplishment. He attempted to smoke the meat to preserve it but found maggots in the meat just a few days after the kill, forcing him to turn the meat over to the wolves. His journal entry confirmed his disappointment with the entire situation stating, "I now wish I'd never shot the moose. One of the greatest tragedies of my life."

In July that year, after a good scratching of the itch, he attempted to return to civilization, but could not cross back over the river due to the Tek being a furiously raging torrent of frigid water and glacier silt. He returned to the safety of the bus without incident and stayed there for the rest of his life.

If McCandless had even a little knowledge of the area or a decent topographic map, he would have known the local terrain, and potentially could have found some easier places to cross the river than his location. Just a short distance upstream the river braids out in a wide plain, while just a little downstream there was a cable crossing the river where the terrain rises and closes into a narrow canyon. Alternatively, he could have just swum for it, though Krakauer notes that McCandless was not a strong swimmer, so the swimming option was likely not reasonable in his mind.

McCandless ended up meeting his demise at the hands of apparent food poisoning, by either eating the wrong seeds or a fungus growing on the seeds due to improper storage in a plastic bag without ventilation. Again, this is a simple mistake that could have potentially been avoided with a little more preparation. It should be noted that the root cause of a paralyzed digestive tract and starvation may be somewhat disputed now. Either way, Alexander Supertramp eventually starved to death in the bus, his body found by moose hunters 19 days after his last journal entry and photo, still wrapped in his sleeping bag. When he was found, his body weighed just 83 pounds.

I have always enjoyed the challenge of a good hike or climb, so the idea of getting to the "Magic Bus," as McCandless called it in his journal, was an adventure I thought I would enjoy. The biggest problem I had was that I lived in Idaho and didn't see a trip to Alaska in my near (or distant) future.

I know you can already see where this is going, so I just remind everyone about a previous comment: the cosmos aligned to present a decision point.

SERE

SURVIVE. EVADE. RESIST. Escape. SERE school was eighteen days of the most intense training I ever attended in the Air Force. The training is not extremely physically exhausting, but the mental gymnastics and mind games are designed to wear a person down. The training is some of the best I've ever completed, but at the same time, given the choice I would never want to endure it a second time. The school was developed many years ago for those who may find themselves behind enemy lines in an effort to get a survivor home with honor. Imagine a pilot who bails out over enemy territory and must orient himself to his new ground situation, establish radio contact with would-be rescue missions, evade the enemy while navigating to the rendezvous point, resist interrogation if captured, and figure out a way to escape confinement in order to effect rescue. SERE school packs all of that into 18 intense days. Now imagine that same person is from the inner city and has never spent one day in the wilderness.

The Air Force Handbook governing SERE school is hundreds of pages thick. As I recently thumbed through the pages,

I recognized how thorough and complete the training really was. Even reading the table of contents would help prepare a person for survival. At the very least, it would be a starting point so the survivor could, at least say, "Yes, I've heard the word *fire*". The Handbook covers everything: what to eat and not eat, how to find water, the importance of good rest and sleep, how to build a shelter, fire fundamentals and importance, biting insects, poisonous insects, wildlife avoidance, map reading, topography, navigation with and without a map in day or night, water crossing and survival, psychology when isolated, combating boredom, positivity, how to set and reach measurable goals—just to name a few.

The first few days of the training are meant to teach basic survival skills using only items you bring with you or would have in an ejection seat. For example, there are no tents, no comfy air mattresses, no Beats headphones. The instructors limit what you can bring to a list of required items like sleeping bags, a canteen, a single gallon zip lock of snacks. On top of that sort of stuff, the trainee may bring clothes and any other items they deem necessary. The cutline between essentials and non-essentials becomes the weight of the pack you carry. Though a major goal of this phase of training is to teach basic minimalist survival skills, there is also a navigation component. Each day and some nights, there is a navigation objective. Trainees are constantly on the move. It was not a big deal to cover multiple miles per day over the rugged terrain of northern Washington, outside Spokane.

I had the added pleasure of attending the training in January when the high temperature in the mountains dropped to the teens. On the first day of the wilderness-training phase, we all had to figure out how to wear and use snowshoes, build a camp, split wood without an axe, and build various types of shelters. The school gave us a single parachute to utilize as we saw fit. After first building a fire for radiant warmth and ambient light, we cut up the parachute into usable sections and began making small shelters for our entire group, which was about 10 people. Each shelter was to be a different style, and capable of sheltering two people, so one of my teammates and I made a "lean-to" shelter out of a couple of dead trees, some branches, and boughs. My survival buddy and I slept in that shelter that night in our mummy bags on top of a thin layer of pine boughs, snuggling nuts-to-butts for warmth. I am not the least bit bashful to admit I've snuggled with another grown man. The temperature that night was negative 17 degrees.

There is no way to escape that kind of cold. In fact, during the night I had to pee really bad, but there was no way in hell I was getting out of my Kelty mummy-style sleeping bag. The closest thing I could figure to use for a pillow was my government issued Gore-Tex jacket, and I suddenly remembered I had stashed a few small, sandwich-sized Zip Lock bags in one of the breast pockets. Tossing and turning in the limited space and doing my best to not wake my snuggle-buddy, I retrieved one of the bags, rolled on my side and with the help of my headlamp and a little luck, managed to pee in that Zip Lock. Have you ever tried to pull two inches of frozen wiener out of four inches of clothes? Next to impossible. When I was finished, I set the bag of pee outside my sleeping bag and went back to a frigid sleep, cuddled once again like a toddler who just had a bad dream. A few hours later when I woke up that bag of pee that had previously been 98.6 degrees was frozen like a rock. That's cold man.

Along with only a couple of others in my group, I didn't really have too hard of a time during this phase. In fact, other than the sleeping temperatures, I found it to be a lot of fun. We didn't have a lot of food or water, but we had a good time completing the various challenges the instructor threw at us. Feet of snow covered the landscape in all directions. The only sources of warmth were huddling together and the occasional fire when we stopped for long enough. Other than that, we had to keep moving to generate body heat. Our group had one chap whose feet would painfully freeze up every time we stopped, so my buddy and I would place his bare feet on our bare bellies to warm him up. Yeah Dennis, that really sucked.

At night we told stories around a campfire when we weren't navigating through the woods in the dark. By day we marched and hiked, singing songs to pass the time. We learned little things like a small candle under a poncho will make you so hot you will be coming out of your clothes, and a cup of instant coffee you'd spend an hour making with snow and a Sterno fuel can may be the best cup of coffee you'd ever taste.

One morning, while in a hideout under my poncho, or "improvised shelter", I melted snow in my canteen cup over a Sterno fuel can. As the snow melted, I whittled a stick into a spoon shape and dug all the moss, dirt and shit out of what was now water. The night before I had scavenged several packs of instant coffee and hot chocolate from discarded MREs, and I added all of it to the water, making myself one of the best cappuccinos I'd ever had. Truly, it was probably disgusting, but it kept me busy for over an hour, and I was proud of my ingenuity and creativity.

The best, most tangible benefit of the course is that they can take a guy (or gal) from the inner city and teach him enough in a few days to survive, for at least a short time, alone in bad-guy land. This basic survival training turned out to be a major source of our false confidence in preparation for a weekend camping trip but was also a lifesaver during our trip to the Bus. One guy in our hiking trio was the very type I speak of: an inner-city kid who had spent more time picking his boogers than time in the woods. Not a dumb guy, by any stretch, and in crazy good physical shape, he simply didn't have the same level of outdoor experience. Love you Banzai.

BREAKING SHIT AND KILLING PEOPLE

"Fighter pilot is an attitude. It is cockiness. It is aggressiveness. It is self-confidence. It is a streak of rebelliousness, and it is competitiveness. But there's something else—there's a spark. There's a desire to be good. To do well; in the eyes of your peers, and in your own mind."
—COL. ROBIN OLDS, FIGHTER PILOT

ENLISTED IN THE Air Force in 1997 following two and a half years of a failed college career at the University of North Alabama. The school and I had differing opinions, and I definitely had a misunderstanding when they said, "Go to school" because I did not associate that with "Go to class." So, I parted ways with college life in favor of the Air Force. I spent my first three years at Tyndall AFB, just outside Panama City, Florida, as an F-15 mechanic—a crew chief. I met my wife, had a son, and eventually received military orders sending my family and me to Elmendorf AFB, Anchorage, Alaska.

Attempting to take advantage of the long hours of dark and cold when there wasn't too much else to do, I went back to school, completed three college degrees and applied to Air Force Officer Training School to be a Maintenance Officer. I figured since I was an aircraft maintainer it would be the most sensible transition—to leverage my knowledge of the maintenance community as an officer. For reasons unknown to me, the Air Force called me and asked if I wanted to fly, and offered me a position as a navigator. After a few quick Google searches, I discovered that I could earn a spot as a F-15E Strike Eagle Weapons Systems Officer, or WSO (pronounced "Whizz-o"). The Strike Eagle, a deep-interdiction, all-weather, two-seat fighter, designed by God and built by man, was at the top of the Air Force fighter jet pyramid, so I signed the commitment letter and began my officer and flight training soon after.

Air Force WSO training begins at Naval Air Station (NAS) Pensacola, Florida. I moved my family back to the Gulf Coast and spent the next year and a half going through flight school. Every pilot or WSO that earns a fighter slot (F-15, F16, F-22, A-10, etc.) must go through two months of training called Introduction to Fighter Fundamentals, or IFF, after receiving his or her wings.

IFF was held at multiple locations at the time I went through, and I attended at Moody AFB, Georgia in the fall of 2006. This training is focused and centered on learning how to fly T-38 jets at over 400 knots, do formation flying, and perform basic fighter maneuvers. It includes rudimentary introductions to air-to-ground bombing, as well as fighter pilot culture and proper etiquette and decorum to help us survive as young fighter aviators in a combat fighter squadron. Sitting in the briefings on the first day, I met a boisterous, stocky young man full of energy and vigor named Ray who would later earn the call sign Banzai.

Banzai and I didn't really hang out too much during that phase of training, but he was slotted to be a Strike Eagle pilot, so our paths were destined to cross in the future. The only interaction I really remember with Banzai during IFF was graduation. Banzai is legitimately one of the most cerebral and intelligent people I know, but he had taken his share of hits in the 2-month course. He still had one flight remaining in the syllabus, and he wouldn't get his diploma if he didn't pass. Failure of the course meant he would lose his fighter slot and end up flying cargo planes full of rubber dog shit out of Hong Kong. Having spent a year in China earning his master's degree, learning the culture well, and speaking Mandarin, I guess it wouldn't be the worst thing to happen to him. Still, the instructors at IFF audaciously presented him his diploma then promptly took it back just to make him the butt of a shitty joke. Banzai flew the next day, passed the flight with flying colors, and continued his path to becoming a fighter pilot.

A couple of months later, I moved into base housing at Seymour Johnson AFB, North Carolina, the home of F-15E Strike Eagle training. Immediately across the street, ushering movers in and out of a moving truck, was Banzai. He, his wife, and son were moving into the house right across from my wife, my three sons, and me. We introduced our families and instantly became friends. In fact, that day during family introductions, Banzai's wife yelled at my wife that my middle son (who was 5 at the time) was peeing on the tire of her

Mercury Mountaineer. I guess that was prophetic enough for us, and we all instantly bonded.

Banzai and I spent the next nine months learning how to break things and kill people, employing the world's best fighter jet, and both received orders to our first operational base at Mountain Home AFB, Idaho. When we arrived in December 2007, we learned we would be assigned to the same squadron as well, the 391st Fighter Squadron, Bold Tigers.

The 391st Bold Tigers have a distinguished history of leading the combat air forces, and Banzai and I were very proud to be part of a decorated squadron with such a long lineage. The impact of that history hit us when we learned the squadron was scheduled to deploy to Bagram AB, Afghanistan, in August, so our sole focus for the immediate future was to get certified for combat and prepare for our first deployment. Within six months of beginning combat-mission-readiness training we would be flying real combat missions, dropping real bombs to protect real good guys from real bad guys. There was a sign in one of the squadron ready rooms that read "The mission is an 18-year-old with a rifle," and we took that very seriously. Another sign posted above the door leading out to the parked jets stated, "DANGER CLOSE, DON'T FUCKING MISS". Wow, no pressure, right?

In May that same year, a new class of young fighter pilots and WSOs showed up to the Bold Tigers, and with it a tall, thin and wicked smart WSO named Matt. Matt had followed a slightly different path to the Bold Tigers, but if there's one truth about the military it is there is no single path to the top. Everyone must figure their own way and what works for them. As Chief of Staff General Mark Welsh use to say,

"Every Airman has a story." The squadron was still in full deployment spin-up mode and Matt was thrust right into it as a young WSO.

Matt had been assigned to the Bold Tigers following a three-year assignment flying EA-6B Prowlers with the Navy at NAS Whidbey Island in Washington State. A seasoned aviator with a rabid appetite for learning and a history of high performance, Matt was selected as one of only two in his class to follow a short check out program and deploy with the squadron in August. Again, no pressure, right?

The deployment went off without much incident. We dropped a lot of bombs, saved a lot of lives and broke a lot of the bad guys' things. Leaving Afghanistan was bittersweet, but we all desperately wanted to get back home to our families. The journey back home took over a week, and during a two-day stopover in Qatar on our return trip, Matt earned the callsign Smokus.

During the deployment, the wives back home set up a solid support network and took care of each other and assisted with family business. My wife became very good friends with Smokus' wife during this time, so when we returned from Afghanistan in January, Smokus and I began to spend quite a bit more time together simply due to our wives hanging out more. Matt and I had been social and friendly during our deployment and always got along well, but the months following the deployment helped us hone in on our shared passion for the outdoors, hiking, camping and adventure. Growing up in Oregon, Smokus was no stranger to the outdoors for sure.

A few months after returning from Afghanistan and in a concerted effort to get back to a complete mission mindset of both air-to-ground and air-to-air excellence, our squadron elected to participate in Exercise NORTHERN EDGE 2009 in Alaska. This trip to Alaska in June 2009 was a TDY, or temporary duty, and was scheduled to be just three weeks long. On a somewhat routine schedule, the Air Force puts on large force exercises in a few different locations. The grand-daddy of them all is Exercise RED FLAG conducted at Nellis AFB, Nevada, near Las Vegas and is likely the most famous of the Air Force large force exercises. It was brought to life after Vietnam when Generals realized the Air Force had not exactly perform to the peak of its capabilities. The idea behind RED FLAG and other large force exercises is to give aircrew of various platforms exposure to combat-like scenarios to teach them how to perform in the fog of war. Hopefully a fighter pilot "dies" during RED FLAG, in an exercise, learns his lessons and doesn't repeat them in true combat when there are real missiles flying back. Exercise NORTHERN EDGE is a bit less grand than RED FLAG but is still comprised of hundreds of aircraft and warriors training for the real thing.

For our exercise, we were to deploy to Eielson AFB, AK just outside of Fairbanks in support of Exercise NORTHERN EDGE 2009, a biennial exercise executed only in odd years beginning in 1975 under the name Exercise JACK FROST. The scope of the exercise is to gather units from all over the pacific theater of operations in order to train tens of thousands of personnel in a joint environment in some of the most complex mission sets the Air Force may face. Army, Navy, Air Force, and Marines all participate and conduct missions together. Troops of any branch do not normally train on such a high level requiring the massive amounts of

coordination required at NORTHERN EDGE, so the opportunity to integrate is seldom passed over. This particular
exercise in 2009 was almost exclusively an air-to-air war
fought over the Gulf of Alaska. Part of the allure of hosting
an exercise in the largest state is the volume of training space
provided. The over-land training space covers nearly 65,000
square miles, while the Gulf of Alaska restricted space offers
another 120,000 square miles of sea and air space.

Mission planning sessions for these multi-ship fights is
intense and laboriously detailed, mostly taking place the
day prior with planning cycles lasting anywhere from 8–12
hours. Monday morning missions were planned on Sunday
afternoons. The airspace was about an hour flight from the
base and aircrews had to air-refuel multiple times to get to
the airspace, fight, and return to base, causing each flight
to last 3–4 hours. We were still considered young aviators
at the time, so it was not uncommon for us to fly every day.
Smokus and I were on the first shift, flying in the morning,
but Banzai was on the second shift, flying until late in the
evening. Though the flight may have been over at 1900 or so,
the debrief normally lasted until midnight most nights.

Now you can see how this situation is starting to frame up.
The three of us flew all week, worked long hours, and were
generally exhausted. Adding to our hiking dilemma was the
fact that Banzai couldn't get away until almost midnight
Friday night/Saturday morning. Then we had to do it all
again the next week beginning with a work call for mission
planning on Sunday at 1600, back at the squadron building.
We were trying to cram this hiking trip into roughly 40
hours. The drive alone took three-plus hours just to get to

the trailhead from the base, located 26 miles southeast of Fairbanks. Three and a half hours there and three and half hours back, plus time for a shower and eat some food when we got home, left us right around 30 to 32 hours to hike the Stampede Trail to the bus. We had to haul ass with minimal sleep, very little food, and no cell phones or Google maps. At this point, if my son had asked me to go on a trip like this, I would have said no. It was shaping up to be a perfect storm of stupidity, bad decision making, and the forces of Mother Nature with us, smack in the middle.

IDEAS AND PLANS

I HAVE AN IDEA. My idea is to build my own house on 30 acres with a pond so I can go fishing whenever I want. I will have a long gravel drive and a four-wheeler ATV racing track in the front yard. I also want goats roaming around the entire property, so I don't have to mow grass. This is my idea. This is not a plan. Plans require...PLANNING! Step-by-step details on how to get from point A to point B. Too often people have good ideas with no plan on how to formulate that idea into reality. An idea alone is just that. It is not executable. In order to see it through, you need to realize the goal, reverse engineer backwards, identifying all steps required, and formulate a plan to complete each step.

When my middle son was 17, he learned this lesson the hard way, as many of us do. He wanted to go camping with three of his friends for his birthday at a lake close by our house. On the surface, I have zero problems with him going out with his friends. I love the idea that they want to get outside and enjoy nature with no cell phones and copious amounts of stories, campfire television, and sunshine. As we neared the weekend prior, I suggested to him he should come up with a good plan and make sure everyone in his party understands that plan.

This would be his first unsupervised camping trip, so I knew there would likely be holes in the plan, and I was prepared to have the conversation with him to help fill in the gaps. Instead of a well-formulated-to-the-best-of-his-ability plan, I got from him, "We're just gonna go camping."

"What are you going to eat?"

"Food."

"Where are you going to sleep?"

"Tent."

"What are you going to do during the day?"

"Stuff."

I decided to take the path of least resistance and allow him the opportunity to experience failure on his own terms. Not so I could say, "I told you so" at the end, but so he would learn a valuable lesson the hard way and hopefully not make that same mistake again. Also, I thought it would be hilarious for him to have to crawl up to my campsite to ask for wieners and buns because their idiot selves only brought a box of Goldfish for three days of sustenance.

As it turns out, he came to me the Wednesday before the trip with his notebook in hand and his tail tucked, asking for help. We went through the play-by-play of packing, setting up, having fun, eating, cooking, sitting, and sleeping. Each of those topics garnered discussion on the who, what, when, where, why, and how. He quickly realized his ignorance and arrogance, took a big bite of humble pie, allowing him to take inputs, make lists, divide duties, and execute. This is a PLAN. He began with the idea.

I fell into the same trap as my son when I decided it would be a good idea to hike to the Bus. I had a good idea (in my opinion), but I didn't really have a plan on how to make it happen. I remember sitting in my dorm room at Eielson AFB after work, researching camping and hiking in Alaska. This is where I remembered my fascination with the Magic Bus. Without hesitation, I unilaterally decided that was our destination. I found Banzai and Smokus the next day and let them in on my plan (idea). Overall, the route fit our criteria perfectly. So I figured it would be an easy sell. I remember the conversation with Smokus vividly.

"Smokus, how extreme do you want to get?"
"Moderately extreme to extreme" he replied.
"Dude, we're going to the bus."

That was all the convincing Smokus needed. Convincing Banzai was a little different. He was reluctant at first, but in the end, peer pressure got the best of him, and he gave in.

I assumed the slight lack of resistance to the trip was based largely on their individual ignorance of the shear scope of the venture. I reckoned they had no idea what I was talking about, so they basically just nodded and agreed. After the event, many years later I found out that Smokus had read the book and seen the movie, and was maybe just as stoked about the idea as I was. Still, the issue was that I had pitched it to them without thoroughly thinking it through. Again, I had an idea and no plan.

It was only when I recognized the paradox that I actually began to give due diligence to the entire situation. The first problem was we were arguably unprepared for a journey of this magnitude. Realizing that profound fact, I began to put in the effort to research and plan the trip so the others would be able to enjoy, rather than have to think about it. Smokus volunteered to secure a ride to get us to the trailhead. This task was easier than expected due to the fact that the rest of the squadron was going fishing as mentioned before. With almost everyone gone, the rental cars remaining were plentiful, so he chose a Toyota 4Runner and we checked "Transportation" off the list. Next was shelter and security. Shelter wasn't a real concern at the time because we all agreed we wanted to go "survival school style". No tents, no sleeping bags. Just a space blanket and a knife. Sleep under the stars. Sounds dumb now for sure, but it seemed like a good idea at the time.

I fancy myself as an outdoorsman for the most part. I have never been scared in the wilderness. I have hiked tall mountains, taken long multi-day backcountry camping trips, fished with bears, spent multiple days alone with not much more than what I could carry in a small schoolbook-sized backpack. To say I was comfortable in the woods would be a bit of an understatement. I enjoy it. I love the sights and smells and scenery. From combat patrols in Afghanistan to hiking glaciers in Alaska, I have never been the type to turn down an adventure. I am also usually prepared for the necessities, at a minimum. Backcountry hiking and camping can stress the limits of what you carry with you. Everything takes up room in a pack, and there is always a tradeoff, with the biggest cost being weight. How much you want to carry, and for how long seems to be the constant balancing act. In other words, get rid of the giant Harry Potter book and take a magazine instead. Better yet, chuck it all and take a pocketknife to whittle wood when you are bored.

A great example of this dilemma is portrayed the 2014 based-on-a-true-story movie Wild starring Reece Witherspoon based on the book of the same name. When the main character, Cheryl Strayed, planned her journey, hiking the Pacific Crest Trail from the southern trailhead near Mexico, she was given advice from various sources on things to pack. Getting her pack on her tiny frame with everything recommended to her, was next to impossible. She had so much junk with her it almost killed her. The lesson: if you don't use it every day get rid of it. Downsize and minimize.

Because we were deployed from home, we were only able to bring with us to Alaska what would fit into a small suitcase or duffle bag. Even before leaving Idaho, I had made choices on what is essential for any hiking/camping trip and what was optional. The cut wasn't easy. Do you take the tent? Back up pair of shoes? Sleeping bag? I ended up with a short list of items that would fit into my daypack because I could not possibly bring my big backcountry pack. I carried a space blanket for emergency warmth, rain proof pants, my Kabar knife and Leatherman multi-tool, hiking shoes, Nalgene water bottle, pocket-sized first aid kit, iodine tablets, a lighter, and a water purifier. That's really the only dedicated hiking and camping gear I brought. I already had some warm clothes as part of my regular packing list: hiking shoes, long socks and liners, moisture-wicking hoodie sweatshirt, cargo shorts, web belt, hat and beanie, and gloves. With the addition of a couple of items, I thought I would be properly outfitted to attempt a "survival school style" trip. Worst case, I figured I'd build a fire and stay warm, then head home. Sleep was optional.

Benjamin Franklin famously said, "Three may keep a secret if two of them are dead." One person. That's it. Any more than that and what was once a secret will eventually be out for public consumption. That is exactly what happened with our plan/idea to go to the bus. Within a day or so of our final decision, everyone in our squadron knew of our idea. Everyone said we were stupid and poo-pooed the idea. Not one single person we talked to about it thought we could make it. Did they know something I didn't? Had they some inside scoop on the weather or area forecast? No, they were just being negative. We were not deterred in the least. If anything, the doubters fueled us with even more motivation just to prove them all wrong. The one person who actually got a vote, versus just being an asshole, was our Squadron Commander. He was the one person who set the rules on how far we could go and what we could do on a given weekend. In other words, he lays out the boundaries of what is acceptable and not.

The Commander approached me in the hallway several days before our planned departure with a list of concerns. He scolded me for a half-baked idea and told me he was not going to allow us to do it. I vigorously protested until I was able to calm him down so we might have a conversation about it and not just kill the idea without even hearing it out. It took me a little time, but I finally got him to admit his overall concern. He told me "All I know about that bus is, that dude died." With a much more politically correct plea than this, and not in these exact words, I basically told him "Hey asshole, don't just crush this because you are ignorant." He left me with a compromise: if I could plan it out and prove to him we were prepared, and promise him we would not attempt something out of our league, he would allow us to go. YES! Ball's in my court. Burden of proof is on me. I love it. The thing he didn't expect, I guess, was the fact that I over-prepare and hate the idea of not being the smartest person in the room. I will win.

The next day or two I spent countless hours reading topographical maps, studying the area, watching videos on the internet, mapping our route...you know, PLANNING! Maybe he was just being a dick, or maybe he was giving me the push I needed to get into the weeds and plan this sucker out correctly. Either way, the result was the same. I finally planned.

By the time I got back to him, I had a power point presentation prepared with exact times from departure to arrival back at the base, packing lists, maps, pictures, videos, and a written plan and emergency contact info. I had sat for hours at our mission planning stations mapping out our route mile-by-mile. I knew the elevation changes, turns, and bends, rivers and obstacles, landmarks. I had memorized everything. I had also linked up with our life-support section and scored 100 yards of 1000-pound white parachute rope, 100 yards of 550-pound parachute cord, a GPS preloaded with maps of the area, and a PRC-112 radio with both VHF and UHF guard channels pre-programmed (121.5, 243.0). I had made this plan my bitch.

There wasn't much I hadn't thought of, but sometimes you don't know what you don't know. Following my presentation to the Commander he agreed to let us try it. He kept saying, "Roscoe, I know you have lived in Alaska before, but those other two? You have to promise me you'll take care of them and not let anything happen to them." He charged me with making sure Banzai and Smokus were good and well taken care of throughout. I agreed as he requested and left it at that. Another simple rule to life: never pass up an opportunity to SHUT THE FUCK UP. If you've won, don't pontificate. Leave it and move on.

DEPARTURE

FRIDAY WAS A long day for all of us, and there really wasn't any end in sight. Smokus and I had gotten up early at 0600 for our mass briefing with the entire first wave of the exercise. The briefing was in the main auditorium of the Exercise facility and probably had 200-300 people present. I must admit, I couldn't have cared less about that mission. All I was thinking about was getting to the bus! We flew our sortie that morning and debriefed until about 1700 or 1800 Friday afternoon. As stated before, Banzai was on the second go, or afternoon sortie, meaning he wouldn't even land before about 1800. The debrief for that go would easily take him to 2300. Our goal was to depart Eielson AFB no later than midnight knowing we had at least a 3-hour drive to the trailhead.

I can only assume Smokus followed a similar timeline as I for that afternoon. Following the debrief I went back to my room and packed up what few essentials I thought I needed for the entire trip. I knew I needed to keep it light while maximizing the "required" gear, so I laid everything out on the bed and racked and stacked it in priority order: water, shelter, warmth, survival. I would have loved to bring some extras, but I still only had a small daypack with me. I bought this pack in 2001 for my wife to hike with me when we lived in Anchorage. Cheap and light, it was a basic Fred Meyer's special. I honestly don't even know the name brand. Of note, I still have this pack loaded and ready to go. It's basically my camping and four-wheeling bug-out-bag, always loaded with a bottle of water, fire starter, baby wipes, first aid kit and headlamp, at a minimum.

As evening turned to night, we realized we needed to get some food before departing. The three of us chose to meet up at the chow hall on base to load up on calories prior to hitting the road. I remember distinctly, Banzai being still fired up about his flight. Whether it was good or bad is moot, but he may have been burning more calories in his fit of rage than he was ingesting. We ate for a bit and chatted with friends and co-workers who had joined, but around midnight we gathered up to leave in accordance with the plan. As we said our farewells and walked out, I grabbed a couple of granola bars and some oatmeal packets from a rack near the door. Just as I stepped out the door I realized I had not packed a pot to boil water.

Our sole means of staying on top of hydration was my Katadyn water purifier/filter and packing a large pot to boil water would have taken too much room. Upon this realization, I snuck back to the kitchen and found a low-ranking Airman that looked like he could give less than a shit about anything, especially cooking breakfast in an Alaskan chow hall at midnight on Friday night. I explained the situation in ten words or less, explained why I needed a pot and begged him to please loan me something to prepare water in. The young man handed me a 4-inch square metal serving bowl from the salad bar that likely held chopped ham or onions or cheese just hours prior. Beggars can't be choosers, so that'll have to do for now. We left the chow hall excited and tired, but our journey hadn't even really begun.

I once drove from Grand Junction, Colorado to Fort Campbell, Kentucky in a 22-hour straight shot. The road trip is easy, following I-70 almost the entire way through Colorado, Kansas, and Missouri. I stopped about every three hours, or so, to stretch, pissed in Gatorade bottles, and drank lots of water and coffee, but the road trip was easy. Interstate 70 from Denver to St Louis is a decent road and fairly straight for the most part. I just set the cruise control and laid back and listened to XM radio. The Blue Collar Comedy channel was a favorite, but even XM played on a loop. After 12 hours, or so, you start to hear the same bits repeating. I really didn't even get tired until the last 100 miles after a drizzly drive, dodging drunk drivers through St. Louis at 0300 Sunday morning, but by then the trip was a test of endurance and a battle of wills that I refused to lose. Most often, your mind will give up before your body, so I slapped out my self-doubt and got through it. Straight, flat, cruise control, XM radio, laid back in my GMC Z71 crew cab truck, that's the way to road trip. The road from the Eielson Air Force Base to the trailhead on the Stampede Road was not going to be that kind of trip.

DEFENSIVE DRIVING FOR DUMMIES

IN MID-NOVEMBER 2000, my wife, son and I drove from San Antonio, Texas to Anchorage, Alaska in a Chevy Tahoe 4x4, and we had only been in the state for four hours when we were introduced to the inherent dangers of the wilderness. This was well before everyone had smart phones and GPS. We drove the whole trip with a CB radio, road atlas and a copy of Milepost magazine, a mile-by-mile guide to the Alaska Highway. The Alaska Highway, or ALCAN, stretches 1387 miles from Dawson Creek, British Columbia to Delta Junction, Alaska. The Milepost Magazine isn't really a magazine at all. It's a full-up book an inch or more thick, and it details down to the tenth of a mile the sights and features of the entire highway.

We were seven days into the journey when we crossed into Alaska from Canada and continued to the junction where we would turn away from Fairbanks and head south-ish toward Anchorage—Tok, Alaska. On the map of Alaska, Tok is a medium-sized dot indicating it should be a town of relatively decent size. The key word here is relatively. Needless to say, we were surprised when we got there to find only a 3-way intersection and a gas station. As of this writing, the advertised population of Tok is still only 1435, so believe me when I say there ain't shit there. We had driven from Watson Lake, Yukon Territory (mile 612) to Tok (mile 1314) in a single day, and we were spent. Not desperate to drive any more after 700 miles already, our plan had been to stay in town and push on to Anchorage the following day. When we arrived in Tok, the idea of staying the night there started to lose traction and a new idea began to form. We thought we could load up on coffee and chips and push through to Anchorage right then and get it over with. After a short deliberation and pros-and-cons debate, we decided to execute: loaded up on gas, coffee and chips and hit the road south to Anchorage, 318 miles into the darkness of our first Alaskan winter.

The evening sun was slowly setting, marking the end of another early winter day in the Alaskan interior. We were maybe only 80 miles, or so, into the trip outside Tok when we passed a house in the middle of nowhere. A kid was in the ditch next to the road, squatting down like he was hiding, and when we passed, he ambushed our truck with a few snowballs. The roads for this stretch were really good and packed with snow making them smooth so I had been going about 80 miles per hour, but when the kid attacked me with hostile fire I slowed down to around 50 to make sure I could keep focus on the road while yelling expletives about what I'd like to do to him and his parents. At this point, I saw something in the road ahead and slowed a bit more as we approached. As we got to within 100 yards of the mystery object I exclaimed, "Holy shit, it's a moose!!!" I took evasive actions by swerving into the ditch at 30 miles per hour and aimed to pass the moose down the driver's side of the Tahoe.

When our truck was abeam the enormous monstrosity of a mammal, she turned suddenly toward the truck, smashing the driver's side mirror and denting the rear quarter panel as she rolled rearward into the darkness. To this day I swear to Jesus I saw the whites of her eyes, and had it been a Bullwinkle I would have been decapitated. The funniest part of the whole episode was that immediately following the attempted murder of her loving husband, my wife asked me to pull over and check out the truck. Hell no woman, I've already had an attempted hit on me once today by an over-sized hooved land mammal, and you don't know what else is out there!

We continued all the way to the town of Glennallen before stopping, and only then did I realize the damage to the rear of our vehicle. In the remaining 180 miles to Anchorage, we had another moose run out in front of us like he was falling out of control down the mountain. Welcome to Alaska assholes!

This little sitcom began a 20-year-plus running joke with my wife and me: we are the Griswolds. You can't write comedy like this. We had been in Alaska for only four hours and already been attacked by the indigenous wildlife. There are literally people who go their entire lives and don't so much as see a moose, let alone have a close encounter of the first kind like this.

So, what's the moral of the story, kids? Those yellow road signs that have pictures of animals on them mean things. In Alaska, if they say watch out for moose, they absolutely mean it. And that's just one species that frequents the highways or can otherwise kill you. We've seen foxes, bears, porcupines, caribou, and wolverines. All have not a care in the world and clearly assume we built those roads for them. I only told you that story, to drive home the fact that while beautiful, the wilderness is dangerous. Both beauty and danger are what stole my ability to nap on the road trip to the trailhead.

I know I just painted this bleak picture of doom for potential travelers in the Alaskan bush, but make no mistake, the reward is worth the risk. The scenery is nothing short of spectacular. Over every crest and around each curve there seems to be a never-ending panorama of mountains, rivers, and trees. This is where postcards come from.

✦

Between the three of us, Smokus decided to drive, and quiet honestly his willingness to jump on the grenade was fine with me for a couple of reasons. First, I was tired and thought I might attempt to grab a nap on the way down to the trailhead. I figured I wouldn't get many opportunities to sleep in the next 48 hours, so I planned to take advantage of the road trip and grab some shuteye. Second, the scenery was gorgeous. If you haven't gotten a chance to drive through the Alaskan interior, then slap yourself and add it to your bucket list. From the undulating terrain to the various Spruce and Birch trees, rivers and wildlife, the landscape seems to always change but somehow remain uniformly familiar. The road is very rarely straight, and the driver really must remain vigilant throughout. The threats to driving were many, but the main one was wildlife. You never know when something is going to jump out of the woods and possibly end your already long day and once-in-a-lifetime trip you hastily planned up.

The road from Fairbanks south is Alaska Highway 3, also known as the George Parks Highway. According to the Milepost Magazine (online), the Parks Highway covers 362 miles through the Alaskan interior from Fairbanks to Anchorage. It was originally called the Fairbanks-Anchorage Highway but renamed in 1975 to the Parks Highway in honor of George A. Parks, the territorial governor from 1925 through 1933. The route is the most direct access to Denali National Park from both the north and south, with the entrance to the park located 125 miles south of Fairbanks. The road from Fairbanks initially turns west for a few miles and curves back south aimed at the small town of Nenana. I refer to Nenana as a small town, but on a map of Alaska it is a "medium dot." Boasting a whopping population of 365 (2017 numbers), it is also the confluence of the Tanana, Nenana and Teklanika Rivers.

The Tanana River is tied for the third longest river in Alaska flowing 584 miles into the Yukon River, the longest river in the State (the 702-mile Kuskokwim River is number 2). The Tanana River Drainage covers most of the interior of Alaska draining almost 46,000 square miles of land. In other words, it's a big river. The Nenana River is quite a bit smaller at only 140 miles in length. The Nenana River flows generally north from the Nenana Glacier in the Alaska Range, follows along the Parks Highway for much of the length and ultimately empties into the Tanana River in the "medium dot" township of Nenana. Just upstream (south) from the Tanana-Nenana River confluence is the Teklanika, or the Tek. The Tek is fed from the Teklanika Glacier in the Denali Range and is located west of the Nenana River flowing north until it eventually drains into the Nenana just a few miles south of the town. This simple knowledge of the local area may come into play later in the story, so just file this away for now.

In addition to the raw beauty of the landscape, there is an element to this drive that further nibbles away my ability to nap. We departed Eielson AFB at midnight Friday September 19, 2009. This was just hours before the summer solstice, the longest day of the year. Many people have heard that in Alaska the sun never sets and I am here to affirm it is true. The sun doesn't set so much as it just dip below the horizon for a couple of hours leaving perfectly illuminated nights especially around the summer solstice. The farther north you travel, the longer the sun is above the horizon. According to almanac data, the sun "set" at 0024 on Saturday morning and "rose" at 0330 local Alaska Standard Time. That's 20 hours and 54 minutes of daylight with the sun actually visible. Due to the sun just dipping down a bit before showing its face at 0330, the drive down didn't even require headlights. This was both good and bad. We were able to enjoy the splendor and grandeur of the Alaskan landscape, but we were not able to get that much needed nap. Humans are not nocturnal creatures, especially when they have been training on an early schedule for weeks. Sleep deprivation would become a factor before the weekend's end.

Approaching the metropolis of Nenana, we had a chance encounter with the locals. Rounding a bend in the road, a cow (mama) moose and her two calves (babies, gender neutral) ran out of the woods and into the road. As if they were travelers that just changed a flat tire, they just pulled out and merged into traffic, running in our lane the correct direction for a couple of hundred yards. Smokus did not see the impending doom that I did—he had not experienced nor witnessed a malicious moose attack of a civilian vehicle before. Just as we neared the three potential terrorist moose they broke hard right into the woods from where they came. As I wiped the sweat from my brow knowing the potential carnage we certainly just narrowly avoided. I spoke not a word, and we continued south.

The Parks Highway south of Nenana flattens and straightens out a bit as it winds its way through the Alaskan interior following the Nenana River Valley. As we traversed the undulating hills from Nenana to Healy the scenery took on a different flavor. Rather than twisty roads carving through lush, forested boundaries, the trees parted in places offering an almost unimpeded view from the north of the Alaska Range, before the road bisects the range between the towns of Healy in the north and Cantwell in the south. Past Anderson, and just a couple of miles north of Healy, we were staring intently at the raw beauty of the mountains when Smokus caught a glimpse of a small, blue road sign in his peripheral vision and hit the brakes—Stampede Road.

Stampede Road is decent paved road until 8 Mile Lake, which is, wait for it, 8 miles from the turn off of the Parks Highway. Normally we would have gone the full distance to the lake and parked there, but for a couple of reasons we stopped about a mile short, parking in roughly a 50-meter square staging area, likely used for people to unload horses, Jeeps or ATVs in preparation for heading the rest of the way out. First, the road turns fairly quickly into a rough, four-wheel drive road within close distance of the lake, and we wanted no part of that. Second, and tied to the first, we were in a rental car paid for by the taxpayers. Though it was on the government's dime, we didn't want to leave another piece of four-wheeled wreckage in the Alaskan wilderness. We figured it would only add a couple of miles to our round trip, so we deemed it not a big deal and stopped.

A JOURNEY OF 1000 MILES...

AFTER RIDING IN the SUV for around three hours, or so, we were all eager to get out and stretch a bit. I, for one, was anxious to get started on our hike, partly because I had been thinking about this non-stop for a couple of weeks now, and partly because I was worried about our time limitations. We were required to be back at the Air Force Base no later than 1600 on Sunday in order to plan Monday's mission. As Smokus turned the car off, we couldn't help but notice it was bright daylight now, and the view of the Alaska Range to the south was magnificent.

The foreground was more rolling, undulating terrain of the taiga and tundra. Blotted with patches of spruce, birch, willow and alder trees, the low-lying underbrush created a carpet-like cover for almost as far as the eye could see. The backdrop was the Alaska Range. Sharp, saw-tooth mountains, almost completely barren except the bright white snow caps, and free of visible life forms, the Range rises above the 2700-foot tree line, creating dramatic vertical significance from our vantage point only a few miles away. The dark, majestic, snow-capped mountains loomed behind the various shades of green making up the lower landscape, and that morning they were capped with a thin layer of clouds floating like whipped cream on a brownie. To borrow the words of Alaskan bushman Glenn Villeneuve, the contrast of rocky, lifeless mountains and lush rolling hills was like "Walking around in a painting." You cannot believe how the scenery there can make you feel small unless you've seen it firsthand.

Opening the doors and stepping out of the car we were surprised by another element of the journey we hadn't really considered yet (the first of many instances). It was fucking cold, man! I don't remember looking at the digital temperature in the car, but almanac data says it was roughly 45° at 3:30 am on Saturday. After sitting comfortably in our shorts and t-shirts for the ride, we could now see our breath, we were covered in goose bumps, and my nipples were hard. Without a bulk of dialogue between us, we all moved toward the rear hatch of the SUV and began the process of dressing for the elements and bundling up in layers. An ancient Chinese proverb tells us, "The journey of 1000 miles begins with one step," so it was time to get out of the car and strap it on boys. We're going to the Bus!

We each took a few minutes to get our minds around what was about to happen. The three of us hadn't really briefed this trip between ourselves too much, and quite honestly, I'm not sure we really knew what to expect in its totality. I mean, I had a pretty good idea, or at least I thought I did, but I'm confident the other two were kind of just along for the ride for the most part. After a few minutes of prep, packing, and layering up clothes, we were ready to begin.

Filled with happiness and excitement and grinning from ear to ear, we took a few happy snaps with the lake steaming in the background, and set out hiking from the parking area. Smokus did not have a camera so he begrudgingly obliged Banzai and me with our picture fetish. We departed the parking area just after 0330 on Saturday morning, and we had all been up since 0600 on Friday...21.5 hours for who-ever's counting.

I grabbed my camera to begin what Banzai and I called our video diary and began filming as we started to walk. I tried to pan around, describing the scenery and each of us as I moved. As I narrated the video, I mentioned, "The trail begins over there." Almost intelligible in the background you can hear Smokus say, "Yeah, the trail of tears."

The first mile or so wasn't too bad. We enjoyed small talk, almost completely centered on complaining about the temperature, but overall, the walk was level and smooth going. We followed the road between the trees and began to encounter an increasing number of deeper and deeper pot-holes, which turned into road-wide mud holes, which turned into running water flowing down the road. At first it was easy to maneuver around these obstacles, but as the road descended slightly into the trees the water holes in the road grew larger and more frequent.

Anyone who's been on a hike of any distance can testify to the criticality of keeping your feet dry. Walking in wet shoes or socks is almost a cardinal sin of hiking in general, so we deliberately attempted to avoid the water and mud at all cost. Well, snowflakes, nothing is free. Our detours took us not only away from the road in many cases but cost us a ton of precious time. Looking back, I estimate we spent roughly an hour to go only about a mile or so. At this snail pace, we might as well just head back to the car, grab a beer and go home.

Not only was the road sloppy, the tundra on either side provided zero relief from what would become a general theme for the following hours. Stepping off the dirt road meant stepping into peat moss and muskeg at least a foot thick. Some was dry, some was not, and we had no way of knowing really until we stepped in it. Couple this with the dense underbrush of alders and willows mixed with flowers and moss, and we were making tortoise-like speed so far.

The Stampede Trail (it's not really a road anymore) was built in the early 1900s to service gold and eventually antimony mines deep in the Alaskan bush. It is just wide enough for maybe a Jeep Wrangler or small SUV to go down, and begins as a pot-holed road resembling an out-of-use logging route. The new problem we were about to face was simple one of evolution. Mother Nature had decided she'd had enough, and took the road back from humankind. What I'm sure used to be a perfectly passable road had now become running water. The creek had taken the road back.

As we approached this section of the trail, we had a real discussion about how important this trip was to each of us. We bushwhacked for several minutes trying to step around the creek, hopping on logs and rocks in a futile attempt to remain dry. One of our videos shows Banzai traversing an 8-foot section of creek by stepping on some rocks. He managed to splash a little water on his feet and legs and noted how (expletive deleted!) cold it was.

Decision point. There was no way in hell we were going to make it to the bus at this rate, and we were growing more and more exhausted and frustrated trying to maneuver around the brush and mud with each obstacle. We could either continue our present tactic or chose the alternative and just go for it and get it over with. We knew we were going to get wet eventually in the river, so why not? We chose the latter and plunged into the ice cold, flowing water of the creek. After the initial shock of freezing cold water getting into our perfectly cozy socks and shoes, it wasn't too bad. In retrospect, it probably really sucked, but our feet were red and numb, so we just stopped caring. We had lost feeling in our lower extremities anyway.

The next few miles continually challenged us with the holistic Alaskan cold and wet experience. We spent a great deal of time stopped, alternating between bundling up and drying out. At one point, we had to pull over for Banzai to fish out his single pair of gloves from the very bottom of his pack. Seriously, it's like he was packing and said, "Yep, I'll need these, let me throw them in here first so they are in the least accessible place when I really need them."

Notice I haven't really referenced Smokus since turning the car off. Smokus is a bit of a quiet guy, and he seemed decently prepared physically and mentally. Maybe he was just taking it all in, or maybe he was frozen from the neck up. Either way, he slogged on with minimal input to the conversation apparently content with his fate at this point. Bigfoot could have snatched him off the trail and Banzai and I probably would have walked another mile before we even knew he was missing. You know, because we're total bros and all.

The road had become the creek and the creek had become the road. When originally built, the Stampede Road followed along Fish Creek as it cut through the tundra toward the Savage River. I'm sure the engineers thought it a good idea when it was graded in, but erosion and time has a way with these things. The Stampede Road had only existed for around a century, and in that time Mother Nature had taken it back. Entropy is king, after all.

Fish Creek, while not powerful by any stretch, took the path of least resistance and made the road its bitch. Unbeknownst to us at the time, the meandering trail had long since parted ways with the road depicted on the map. By diligently studying the topographical maps of the road, I had determined the distance to the bus to be right about 14 miles one-way. Due to the trail changing course over time, the actual distance was closer to 20 miles one-way, another gross miscalculation on my part. Who the hell put me in charge?

Along the way we passed a couple of campsites that seemed to be abandoned, but could be usable with a little TLC. One camp was an old truck bed camper set up on blocks only a few feet off the road. We didn't have the balls to investigate, but there may have been goodies in there we could have used later. OK, I know what you're thinking. That's stealing, right? Sure, but there is also the idea of "take-one, leave-one." If you borrow something from a site, leave something of equal value in its place. For example, if you need a pair of gloves, leave a pair of extra socks, or if you really want that can of beans leave a couple of granola packets or something—one-for-one swap.

We continued freezing cold step after freezing cold step, literally walking what felt like miles-at-a-time through the creek in ankle to shin deep freezing cold running water. Almost as abruptly as we entered, miles ago, the trees parted and gave way to wide-open tundra revealing our next challenge.

WARNING: BOYS PLAYING IN MUD

THE ROAD/TRAIL/CREEK WAS densely lined with brush and trees for several miles. At times the walls of thick underbrush and trees were claustrophobic and oppressive. We really couldn't see too far into the forest on either side due to the interwoven vegetation, and looking forward, we could only see as far as the next turn in the road, or creek, as it were. It was like walking in a corridor or canyon of trees similar to the "green tunnel" term hikers used to describe the Appalachian Trail. A major difference in that analogy, and where we stood, was our trail was filled with flowing ice water.

When hiking through elements like this, you are required to focus intently at only about the next six feet in front of you. This intense concentration can lead to a bit of time dilation giving the sensation that as quickly as we entered this part of the trail we exited into a vast opening of tundra. The high and dry ground was now visible in the distance ahead of us, and excitement took over as the emotion of the moment. Stopping for a few minutes, relishing finally being at the point we could enjoy the scenery of Denali to the south, we realized once more everything comes at a price.

After enjoying the scenery and direct sunlight for a short siesta, we marched ahead following the trail. Our joy quickly became anger when we got to the mud—lots and lots of mud. This is the kind of mud that tries to rip off your shoes when you step in and out. The kind of mud that stays on you for a few days. The kind of mud that takes a fresh Brillo pad to scrub off. Mother Nature had apparently decided to join our squadron-mates in trying to induce every obstacle possible to impede progress. There might as well have been an old grey-bearded Gandalf screaming at us with his thunderous wizard voice, "Thou…shall…not…pass!" She not only left us a giant mud bog to cross, but she infused it with peat and muskeg making it a sloshy, mossy sucker hole of doom. I swear I felt like I was in an Indiana Jones movie trying to rescue the stolen artifact from what would certainly cause worldwide destruction, only to be fraught with impassable obstacle after impassable obstacle. This was turning out to be a never-ending problem-solving equation, and I was not in the mood. I just wanted to go for a hike, man.

Several people over the years have documented and blogged their experiences on the Trail more completely than we did at the time. Explaining the view from where we stood in words is next to impossible. Having just exited the trees into the open tundra, we could see rolling hills out to the west ahead of us. In the distance, maybe about one or two miles, was a tree line generally in the direction we were headed. As the "trail" followed Fish Creek to the north and west, to the right, the terrain seemed to be slightly higher elevation. To the south there looked to be endless open tundra plain with a distant backdrop of the Alaska Range.

This vantage point also happened to provide a decent spot to see Mount McKinley to the southwest, still solid white with packed snow contrasting the blackish-brown smaller mountains in front. Immediately in front of us, as if placed there as a warning barrier to soft day-hikers like us, were the mud plains.

During my research for the trip, I had read about the mud bogs as a sort of a landmark along the trail, but until laying eyes on it personally, I could not envision the size and volume. Keep in mind we are hiking in June. During the winter and colder months, the ground in this area is permafrost. No doubt this was the case when McCandless made his journey west down the Stampede Trail. The water and moisture in the muskeg and peat bogs freezes up solid making traversing essentially a breeze. June is a warm month in Alaska and all that permafrost had now melted into a Great-Northwest-Tundra-Peat-Moss-Muskeg-Sticky-Sloppy-Sucker-Hole-Swamp of unknown size and depth. Oh, and the trail all but disappeared becoming ruts and tracks in all directions almost as far as we could see.

Staring at the mud flats we were faced with another decision. How in the hell do we deal with this? Our available solutions were to quit and retreat to the warmth and safety of civilization, try to go around this gigantic quagmire, or blast right through it.

I would not describe any of us as quitters, so option one was right out. We had not reached the point of accepting defeat, just yet. To go around may take us miles off course. We generally knew where the trail was supposed to go, but if we got too far off course, we may spend hours trying to find it, not to mention the calories we would burn in the process. The only feasible way to get to the high ground and stay on track was to traverse this shit hole, and that's exactly what we did. We bailed off into the mud like we had good sense and tried to make the best of it.

So, remember a long time ago, when I told you about trying to keep our feet dry and stuff? Yeah, about that. We began this hike worried about a few inches of cold water. At this point we were no-shit stomping though feet-thick mud and muck. We had mud up to our knees, easily.

Smokus lost balance and fell in the middle somewhere, and I'm pretty sure Banzai and I silently agreed if he didn't get back up, we weren't going back after him. Screw all that "no man left behind" shit. It took too much energy and there's no telling if the tundra wouldn't swallow him up like the Sarlacc Pit in Star Wars. Ashes to ashes, mud to mud, Alaska had him now. I'm sure he'd have become a vibrant flower or something in his next life, but alas, he struggled to his feet and kept moving like a wounded soldier making his way out of the battlefield. His light gray sweatshirt with AIR FORCE displayed proudly on the front in dark blue block lettering, and his khaki Columbia zip off hiking pants were now forever scarred and stained with Alaskan mud.

Escaping the captive grip of the mud was a small victory. Filled with joy, we shook off as much grossness as we could, and moved on toward the higher elevation and drier footing, making our way toward the tree line in the distance. Passing another camp, we could tell this area of the trail was a favorite for travelers to settle in for the night.

One particular camp on the right would have been the

Alaskan bush equivalent to a Holiday Inn Express. Small stacks of firewood were scattered out around a central burn pit. One-foot diameter trees had been cut into short stumps for sitting so campers didn't have to sit in the dirt, and plenty of flat open areas for tents. There were even a couple of barrels to store your belongings overnight to keep them dry and deter bears. The site was high and dry, a condition we were presently envious of, but we did not have time to stop. Onward we walked, squishy step after squishy step.

WINONA'S GOT A BIG BROWN BEAVER

ENTERING THE TREE line once more, the trail abruptly changed from dry and sunny back to shaded, sloppy, muddy and wet. Due to the winding trail, getting off track in the mud flats and following a flowing creek, I had essentially given up on keeping track of the miles. As a total guesstimation based on nothing but a map and gut feeling, I figured we only had a mile or so to the first of two major river crossings, the Savage River. I had read in my research phase of beaver dams along the route that could make the trail quite wet at times, but hadn't really given it much thought except it would serve as another landmark and maybe offer us an opportunity to see some wildlife—gross miscalculation number 69.

As we hiked in what was now dense, lush boreal forest, we noticed the water in the trail was no longer moving like it had previously. To this point in the trip, we had basically been walking in a flowing creek with any water standing in the road just smallish mud holes. The water we were in now seemed different, somehow. Clear, cold and placid, the water resembled the shallows of a pond or small lake rather than a wet road or creek. That's about the time we came to the beaver dam.

The dam wasn't very big, stretching only 15 yards or so, but the ponds it created were formidable to the three of us on foot. We didn't see the beaver itself, but we did see freshly cut trees indicating this was an ongoing project by nature's engineers. The water was cold, but at least it wasn't flowing.

The biggest issue we saw with this obstacle was the fact that we couldn't accurately gage the depth of the water. Crossing was going to be an experiment in how deep and exactly how wet we were willing to get. The sun was still low early in the morning and the shade made the ambient temperature very chilly. Getting wetter at depths unknown was not high on our list of fun things to do at this point.

As if a common theme, we tried to search for ways around the pond first, with zero success. Growing up in the south, I knew enough about beaver dams to know it generally wasn't a good idea to walk across them unless you were very familiar with the area, timber, and age of the dam. Never mind the fact that beavers chew their timber so that each end is as pointy as a Spartan spear, fresh dams tended to be weaker than older dams as beavers continually improve their projects. We knew there were dams on our route, but didn't know where, how many, or when they were made. Crossing the dam would be risky at best. We could always turn around and go home. After all, we were all tired and hungry having burned roughly one-kazillion calories and been up for about 28 hours. Or we could just go for it.

That feeling of getting your junk wet for the first time is a thing in even moderately cool water. Getting your junk wet in a freezing beaver pond in the Alaskan bush is like elite-prestige-expert level. I'm pretty sure my balls retreated to somewhere around Fairbanks trying to get as far away from that water as possible.

Smokus and I are both around six foot three, but Banzai is a bit shorter. No short jokes here, this is serious. Due to his, let's call it low center of gravity, he was the first to wail in shock as his testicles made their way to another dimension. Hilarity ensued, but only for a brief moment as just a couple of steps later Smokus and I felt it. My nipples could have cut glass. I think the beavers engineered the dam to bring the water just up to sack level on purpose, and I will never forgive them for that.

Once the initial shock was over, we waded to the other side roughly 30 yards away. When we got out of the water, our legs were bright red from the near-freezing cold water, and everything from the belt down was shriveled, soaked, or evacuated all together. This trip sucks.

The remaining trek to the Savage River was more of the same, but the water was not as deep as in the beaver ponds. Routinely we crossed long swaths of knee-deep ice-cold water. Though the environment was dark and cold, the beauty was remarkable. Many times, we stopped just to enjoy the scenery. All right, I confess, we stopped to warm up too, but it was still pretty.

The water was so still and reflective, you could see the reflection off the surface as if looking in a mirror. I took a few pictures, but the one I love the most is one of a long patch of perfectly still, standing water in the road. I can turn that picture upside down and you literally cannot tell which end is up. This short stretch of the trail was also the thickest woods of the entire trip. The black spruce and birch trees were dense and blocked out the sun, while the ground was bright green with lush grass, flowers and shrubs.

Approaching the Savage River is anticlimactic. We were so focused on the next few feet in front of us and how cold our legs and feet were, that we just rounded a curve and *Blam!*, there was a river in the way. We took a long break at the Savage to enjoy the scenery and rest. If we'd had any food this would have likely been our lunch break.

Sitting on a log staring at the river I remarked at how unimpressed I was. I had read a lot on the area and about the rivers, both the Savage and the Tek, and I had this idea in my head that crossing the Savage would be at least close to parallel to the Tek. Boy was I disappointed and underwhelmed. While I walked around scoffing—this inferior river that in no way rose to my expectations—Smokus and Banzai enjoyed their break in a slightly different manner.

As I explored the shallows of the puny river/creek/stream, Smokus and Banzai huddled over a map on the rocky bank. They were 100 percent convinced we were lost as hell. I, on the other hand, was equally convinced we were headed the right way. The trail had been a little different than predicted, so their concern was not totally unwarranted. We expected to more or less follow Fish Creek more to the north and west as we approached the Savage. As it turned out, we followed a road with no creek really in sight. The still waters we had just passed through were certainly not what we expected. Still, looking at the map, I was not terribly worried about our current position. Even if we were off just a little, continuing west would run us right into the Tek.

My exact words from our video diary: "Well, we made it to the Savage, and if this is it, I'm truly unimpressed. I mean… I've fished barefoot in worse creeks than this." Continuing to narrate as I panned the camera around to Smokus and Banzai, "These two douche bags think we're lost, I think we're on the right track, whatever. Beautiful out here, though. Might even make camp here, who knows, we'll see."

After a short break, we geared back up and took the plunge into the depths of the Savage River. This river was not a giant obstacle in any way. The water was only as high as just below our knees, maybe slightly higher perceived by Banzai, but only he knows that. We cruised right through without incident and hit the trail on the opposite shore headed to the Tek.

The relatively short distance between the Savage and Teklanika Rivers, only a mile or slightly more, was drier than most land we had been on all day to this point. The trail follows the west shore of the Savage for a short distance before breaking west toward the Tek, crossing a small ridge of high ground in the process, allowing the sun to warm and dry us out. As the trail shallowed and flattened, we began to hear the rush of water, and we soon found ourselves emerging from the forest onto a very rocky and sandy beach. We had made it to the Tek.

THE TEKLINIKA RIVER

GOING THROUGH NAVY Aviation Pre-flight Indoctrina-
tion at Naval Air Station Pensacola, Florida, was a special
experience, and I specifically remember the swimming portion. The curriculum contained an evolution during which
the instructors placed the students in a large Olympic sized
pool with various obstacles scattered throughout. One such
obstacle was "the chair".

The chair sat just above the water so when you sat down
your butt would be barely touching the surface. Below the chair
were two square Plexiglas tubes of some length, maybe 10 to 20
feet, and large enough for a human to swim through. Inside
each tube was a hatch-like door, but only one was open at a
time. The student was told which end was correct, moments
prior to execution of the event. A trainee would sit in the chair,
strap in with a lap belt, and give a thumbs-up to the instructor
who then pulled a lever and the chair rotated 180 degrees on
its longitudinal axis. The legs of the chair were now pointed
toward the sky and the trainee's cranium and upper body was
submerged. He then had to unbuckle and swim to the end that
had the open door at the end of the plastic tunnel.

Disorienting is not even close to the word to describe the sensation when you go under. Everything you knew is now wrong. Left is right and up is down. I might have even pissed my pants and forgot my name.

✦

Turning the corner out of the woods onto that remote Alaskan beach was like turning on the lights in the living room on Christmas morning. That familiar rush of excitement reminded me of childhood, staring wide-eyed at the expertly decorated and lit tree with my presents stacked underneath, the same presents I had been staring at for days wondering what surprise each contained. I guess my emotions were due to the Christmas-morning-like buildup of anticipation, or the physical toil for the last several hours. Maybe it was just the spectacle of it all contrasting sharply with the claustrophobia of the trail. Whatever it was, we were excited for maybe the first time on this trip. We smiled.

If the beach had been made of something other than softball to bowling ball sized smooth river rocks, we might have skipped up to the shoreline like Dorothy skipping down the yellow brick road, holding hands and singing. As quickly as our adrenaline and endorphins raged skywards, mine plummeted to basement levels. Standing slack jawed on the bank of that river I realized the true challenge presented.

For starters, I walked up to the raging torrent, stared in shocking disbelief, and discovered for the first time IT FLOWED NORTH!!! I don't know why I had not noticed this before. I might have been delirious and sleep deprived, but my brain could not get around or comprehend this newly found information. I had read tons of internet articles, Krakauer's book "Into the Wild" twice, seen the movie of the same title, stared endlessly at countless topographical maps, researched and looked at pictures of others' accounts of the trip, yet somehow I overlooked this glaring detail—North, not South. Up is down, left is right, white is black, cats and dogs living together. Mass hysteria. Everything I had referenced and every landmark I'd counted on was now in the opposite direction.

In military tactical aviation we have a code word for this helpless state of mind—tumbleweed. It means you have completely lost all situational awareness and don't know which end is up. The feeling of complete and total disorientation I had standing on the shore with my feet in the Tek staring blankly in a vain attempt to regain my wits was exactly the same as that damned chair in Pensacola. Roscoe's Tumbleweed. God, I'm stupid.

The three of us stood at the edge of the rushing river for quite some time, each contemplating exactly how the hell we intended to conquer this obstacle. Anyone who has heard or read about Chris McCandless, The Stampede Trail or the Magic bus knows this river is by far the largest obstacle impeding success on what would otherwise be a rather benign backcountry adventure. While stationary and surveying in all directions for a possible solution, I was taken back by just how forceful the Tek really is. I had read about it and watched videos, but just like many other sights along this journey, you cannot possibly comprehend its totality until you are standing there staring it down.

When we crossed the Savage just a short time prior, the water was relatively clear, and the flow was not terribly strong. The Tek was completely different. The Teklanika River is a powerful river, flowing north (as I know now) from the Alaska Range. It is fed from a glacier of the same name and the water is freezing cold. During the winter months, the water runs lower and is more of a clear, glacier blue, but this time of year it is muddy and mucky, filled with silt and dirt from far upstream as it stretches its boundaries like a little fat kid wearing last year's clothes. Krakauer describes the river as "latte" color or the color of "wet concrete" in his book. It is indeed light grayish brown with frothy eddies, swirls and rapids. We could not see the bottom even in the shallowest portions.

The color made the river seem to take on a life of its own, especially in relation to its little brother, the Savage. The river also had a voice. As we approached the river and while still in the woods, we registered the sounds of a low roar, almost like the white noise generated by a box fan in a bedroom when you are trying to fall asleep. Getting closer, and still in the woods, the sound grew stronger, lower and more powerful more akin to driving a car with the windows down. Standing on the banks, the raging river was deafening, water splashing into the walls and banks with rapids rolling and boiling the full length across, and the rumbling of rocks beings tossed along the bottom. Even standing just a few feet from each other we had to raise our voices to just under a shout to communicate. Farther upstream, the water braided out into several routes of varying sizes, with edges swelling and billowing against the restraints of the banks. Bushes and small trees that otherwise would have been basking in sunshine were now at least partially submerged and taking a beating from the current. The river looked and sounded angry.

After a few awestruck minutes, we managed to pick our jaws up off the beach and retreat to a clearing farther away from the shouting river and closer to the tree line. The nearby sitting area was fairly well worn, making it obvious we were not the first to sit a spell to regain our composure after first contact with our opponent.

Sitting on a log in the sunshine was not going to get us across this river, so we decided to work our way upstream hoping to find a more suitable crossing point. The most discouraging thing about our exact position was that on the far bank we could see the trail on the other side taunting us like Arnold Schwarzenegger taunting the Predator, "Come on, I'm here, what are you waiting for!!!??"

Rested, we moved 100 yards, or so, upstream to take a closer look at one of the braided sections. I plopped down into the water and eased out into the current up to my knees thinking it wasn't too bad for the moment and this could actually be possible. I stumbled cautiously farther and farther into the murky flow, but I lost my footing near the main current and backed out. Determining the flow was way too swift to cross, we retreated once more.

Banzai and I thought it best to continue upstream in search of a more favorable crossing. Smokus, wanting nothing to do with walking farther or getting wet again, tried to convince us all to return to the sitting area on the beach and make a fire to help us dry out and warm up a little. Recognizing that separating the herd was generally a bad idea, Smokus

caved into peer pressure and we all chose to try a little farther upstream for a good crossing area. As we continued
up the east bank of the river in dense brush and alders, the
thickets eventually gave way to wooded high ground overlooking the river. On this small knoll perched above the river
below we spotted a blue tent, so we gave a wide berth before
continuing up stream to a landing on the side of the water.
We could tell the area had been highly trafficked recently
due to the matted foliage on the bank, but as far as we could
tell there was no way to cross here. The braid was only about
10 yards across and at this specific point there was a small
alder in the middle swaying and straining against the current. We surmised someone must have launched a boat or
sat there fishing or something because no one in their right
mind would get in that water.

I SEE DEAD PEOPLE

A S WE MADE our way back to our initial rest area about 200 yards away, we once more passed the blue tent and swung wide to give ample space and not be a bother to the residents, although there didn't seem to be any signs of life emanating from the area. We neared the point where the braids all met up and formed back into a single stream. The braid was still only about 10 yards across, and if we made it to the island in the middle, we stood a reasonably decent shot at crossing the bigger channel on the other side. It was considerably wider, and we assumed the perceived current would be less. You know, Venturi's principle and stuff, or something like that.

I had already tested the river in several spots, so Banzai decided to jump on the grenade this time. He summoned all his available courage, removed his backpack and stepped into the river. The main current of this particular braid was near the opposite bank and only two or three feet wide. I guess we reckoned we could more or less step over that portion to the far shore. As Banzai moved toward the objective, he executed flawlessly. Using a stick for balance, he leaned into the current facing upstream forming a sort of tripod. As mentioned before, Banzai is smaller in stature, but stocky, very fit and very strong, with good balance. He reminds me of the male gymnasts I've seen on TV. I honestly thought he had it and we were going to the bus. Then, it happened.

Now, I've been an outdoorsy kind of guy my whole life. I've been a card-carrying member of local and county Search and Rescue teams, I've witnessed and been a first responder to horrific car crashes, I even cradled and held a pregnant young lady after her H2 Hummer was t-boned by a minivan full of kids. I served 21 years in the Air Force and did three combat deployments in Afghanistan, twice as an Air Liaison Officer with the 101st Airborne Division in some remote areas. Despite these experiences, I've still only seen the look of sheer terror on someone's face twice in my life.

Over a Fourth of July weekend in Idaho, I had taken my family out camping in the southern edges of the Sawtooth Mountains in the Boise National Forest. We camped for three days near Trinity Lakes and Trinity Mountain, a 9500-feet tall granite mountain overlooking the surrounding forest. Because it is the highest point in the area, the very peak of the mountain is home to a National Forest Ranger Station and serves as a wildfire lookout during fire season and summer months. The road to the lookout is very rough and only suitable for a short wheel based 4x4 truck or Jeep, but it makes a great hiking trail. I had hiked to the top of the mountain several times alone, with Smokus, and with my youngest son, who was five at the time. We enjoyed feeding the ground squirrels granola bars out of our hands, and the views were magnificent.

To wrap up and put a bow on our perfect camping weekend

we decided to hike up to the ranger station and enjoy one last view prior to descending back down the mountain and eventually to home. Even on Fourth of July weekend, we routinely ran into snow along the road up to the lookout. The snow covering the road forced us to park my truck about a mile away and walk the rest. The road crossed a saddle in the mountain and began a steep climb with several switchbacks to the top as it clung to the edge exposing extremely steep, cliff drop offs to the open side. If a person slipped or fell here it was a long, rocky ride to the bottom about 700 feet below.

My youngest son and I were moving right along. We had completed this hike a time or two, and we both wore proper hiking shoes, but my wife and other two sons had never been here before and wore regular sneakers. Hindsight is always 20-20, I know. My youngest and I had rapidly taken the lead and moved about 30 yards ahead of the rest of the group when I heard a scream from the rear party. I turned around to see my wife and oldest son standing on the edge looking down. That's when I realized my middle son was gone.

I ran down to them as fast as I could and found my son a few feet below clinging to the side. As he slipped and slid, he had flipped over on his stomach and dug in his hands and feet for everything he had. He clawed the mountain with every ounce he had and stopped only about six feet down. When he looked up at me, that's when I saw it—the look of sheer terror. He was frozen with fear and must have known his life was in severe danger. He was seven. In that moment I saw him in slow motion, and I felt completely helpless. I snapped out of it, grabbed a nearby stick and lowered it down to my son gathering him back up to the trail; no worse for wear at least on the outside. So you're no doubt sitting there like "Oh my God, you're a terrible father, how could you do that to your child?" You are correct, but wait, there's more.

I have been called a very determined individual at times, maybe even a little bit stubborn. My wife and I discussed our current situation and lobbied our sides to continue or retreat. Finally, my wife pulled the mama bear card and demanded we return to the truck. This trip was terminated, and I could hardly argue. At this point we knew we had lost, so we retreated down the mountain. Recognizing and admitting defeat we began our decent to better trail, and eventually, the truck.

Time compression is a thing. We walked at a slower pace than before being extra careful with our steps and taking the high ground on the trail whenever we could. Suddenly I heard a scream and saw a flash of blonde heading the wrong way falling down the jagged mountain face. When I finally came back to real-time, I saw my wife roughly fifteen feet down the mountain clinging to a one-inch diameter pine sapling. Like my son, she had slipped on the snow and slid down. She later told me as she slid on her butt, she eyeballed that small tree and steered the best she could towards it knowing it was her only hope of evading certain death down the cliff. She spread her legs and took the tree right into the crotch and hung on for dear life. Had she not done this we would have lost her down the mountain, for sure. I carefully stepped over the edge and reached out the same rescue stick for her to get her back up to the road.

My wife eventually took the blame for her misfortune revealing she was looking around rather than focusing on stepping carefully through the snow. She took her eyes off the trail and slipped, simple as that. We were all a bit shaken by then, so we slowed the pace even more, eventually arriving home without further incident. In the span of just a few minutes I had earned "Dad of the Year" and "Husband of the Year" honors. Pick something and be the best, I guess.

✦

Crossing the small braid in the Teklanika River, Banzai measured every step carefully and staggered towards the opposite shore. Smokus and I were still dry on the bank trying to do our best coaching and cheerleading to Banzai when the river stole his footing. His body disappeared for only a brief second before he regained his footing and braced himself on his hiking stick. In that singular moment, I reacted and was poised to go in after him, but he popped back up and looked right at me. There was that look. The look that says, "Tell my wife and kids I love them." That look that pleads, "Please don't let me go down this fucking river and end up in Russia." That moment lasted only a second or two, but felt like an eternity. Carefully, but expeditiously, he made his way out of the river and back to Smokus and me, on the bank. We stood there for a few seconds, analyzing our situation and realizing the peril we narrowly avoided.

Banzai was soaked from the neck down, and I was bent over in shock. Maybe it was adrenaline, or maybe it was the realization that our trip to the bus was now completely thwarted, but we looked at each other and burst out laughing and snapped a ton of pictures of Banzai's near death experience. We even joked that Smokus and I could have just picked him up in Nenana on the way home. "Friend of the Year Award," yes please, I'll take that one too.

After we calmed our nerves, we eventually gathered our packs and returned to the sitting area on the beach near the trail where we initially approached the Tek. Smokus sat on a log and built a small fire. Banzai stripped and tried to dry his clothes. I sulked and pouted like a three-year-old in timeout. We retold the story of Banzai nearly meeting his maker, had a few quick laughs at his expense, and discussed options moving forward. Should we continue to hike around in search of a place to cross, or should we take a short siesta and begin making our way back to the car? Deep down I knew the trip had reached its pinnacle, it was over, but I decided to explore the area anyway. The mid-day sun was ducking behind the growing clouds, but it was warm and we weren't getting wetter for the moment. We were drying out and warming up with every minute, so why not see what else is out there?

DEFEAT

MADE MY WAY downstream to the north from our position, bushwhacking my way through the thick alders and
willows. From the map study I knew the Teklanika-Savage
confluence was just a short distance, and although the banks
of the rivers closed in to form a narrow canyon, I thought
there was a slight possibility of finding a crossing closer to
that area. Additionally, several sources had described a cable
crossing between the cliffs just a few yards in that direction,
as well. If still attached, we could potentially use that to get
across. Even after almost losing Banzai to the river, I per-
sisted that we were not finished. When a door is shut in your
face, kick it open and keep going.

I followed the river to the max extent possible to better
look out for the cable, but the terrain rose and the river narrowed as the canyon walls grew tighter and tighter. The
rapids boiled and the roar from the rush was deafening.
There, hanging limp and lifeless on the side of the cliff wall
was a thick, rusted cable. The cable had been severed and
just dangled on the side, once again taunting me. Alaska was
making me its personal comedy show and I was falling for

it completely—hook, line and sinker. Deflated and beaten, I accepted my lot and returned to Smokus and Banzai, who had by then stripped down to shorts and t-shirts and basked in the sun. Banzai was taking the opportunity to utilize the sun plus Smokus' fire to dry his soaked clothes.

We sat for a long time laughing at Banzai's folly, once more, drying our clothes, and enjoying the Alaskan wilderness. We had not seen another person the entire day, and except for ruts in the mud flats and the single blue tent, we hadn't seen much evidence of humans, at all. I gathered the metal bowl and oatmeal from my backpack and attempted to make us all oatmeal for lunch. We had just a little fresh water remaining, so I decided to just scoop some water from the river and boil it to get rid of any microbes. Smokus and Banzai vehemently objected and refused any oatmeal because of the high silt content of the water. When you get hungry enough you will eat just about anything, and that's what I did. After all, God made dirt, and dirt don't hurt.

As I ate my gritty oatmeal, I reflected over the last few days and hours leading to this exact point. I had put so much energy into this adventure, both physical and mental, that the thought of not reaching our destination had never really crossed my mind. I had visualized sitting outside the bus waiting for Banzai or Smokus to take my picture in the same pose as McCandless. I had seen myself making the video guided tour of the interior. I had imagined every step of the trip in detail as I daydreamed.

Sitting on that stump, drying my clothes by the small fire Smokus had built, chewing apple-cinnamon flavored glacier silt, I was sunk. Losing had never been an option. I am a winner. I will find a way to win. The thought of giving up pulled me down into a depression. This River had grounded me back into reality and strained my ego. Though I tried hard to keep it inside and not let the others see, I was crushed. Deflated. Defeated. But life goes on, and we reluctantly decided to return to the car and admit defeat. The same river that forced McCandless to return to his Magic Bus had now blocked our approach and sent us home with our tail between our legs. The folks back at our squadron are going to love this.

After lunch and some good conversation, we figured if we left soon we could get back to the car and return to Fairbanks by late evening. At the very least we could make it back the Alaskan Holiday Inn camp spot and stay there for the night, so we started to get our things together. Clouds had moved overhead changing the current situation rapidly from sunbathing to bundling up. In this process, Banzai reached deep into his pack and retrieved three cigars. These were to be our victory cigars, smoked only upon reaching the bus. Before we lit up, we wanted to document the moment in video, so I pulled out my camera and started filming Banzai standing in his combat boots, shorts and t-shirt waving a cigar around in the air as a prop.

Roscoe: "Banzai, you may speak"

Banzai: "Oh, why, thank you. So, I brought these three cigars from The Dude's personal collection back home for us to have to go smoke up in a school bus. Obviously, we're not at a bus. But you know what, I think its ok. I think we can still smoke these cigars, these victory cigars. Because we've had a lot of obstacles put in our way, like our squadron who wouldn't fucking let us leave until midnight Friday fucking night, so we've had zero sleep, we're on hour 30 of fucking being awake, we've still got a nine-and-a-half-mile fucking hike to get out of here. We get all the way to this fucking river after beg, borrowing, and stealing everything we can to get here, fucking traipsing through four feet of water, with mosquitoes and probably Ebola, and get to this fucking glacial river that almost has killed us, has killed people before, and I'm sorry, but we can't fucking get past it. I'm not ashamed. Oh, and it just started fucking raining! But you know what, I'm proud of what we've done her today gentlemen. For everyone that said, "I told you so," Fuck them. We did something today. I'm not sure what it is yet, but I'm gonna figure it out. I'm proud of us, God dammit."

Roscoe: "We all got jungle rot on our feet, that's all we did today!"

Not exactly a Doctorate-level use of the "F" word, but still pretty good and articulated our sentiments exactly. Defeat and delirium gave way to hilarity. We were still laughing our asses off when we heard the voice calling to us in the distance.

PHOTOS

Everyone was all smiles at the beginning the trail at 8 Mile Lake.

The trail quickly deteriorated into a creek.

Walking in knee deep freezing water for miles sucks.

Crossing the Savage River enroute to the Teklinika.

Approaching the Teklinka we could see the trail taunting us on the other side.

Trying to find a suitable crossing at the Tek.

Happy faces after Banzai almost went for a ride down the River.

Posing in front of the famed "Magic Bus".

Warming and drying out at the "Magic Hippies'" fire.

My last look at the Teklinika River at 0400 Sunday morning. I was
wearing every stitch of clothing I had and still freezing.

MAGIC HIPPIES

As the rain sprinkled down lightly on our "victory party", we heard a faint voice calling from the south. There, walking up the bank towards us were three young men, each dressed in jeans and flannel sporting weeks-old beards and beanie caps. I don't remember their names, but from the moment we met them we referred to them as "the hippies", and as time went on they cemented their legacy as "the Magic Hippies". They moseyed closer and introduced themselves, "Hey y'all, we saw your fire and thought we'd come say hi." Uhhh, hi? Aside from the tent we thought we were the only ones out here, and even the tent had no signs of life when we passed close by.

We introduced ourselves and made some small talk. The three explained how they were on a sort of "find Jesus sabbatical" from Canada or something. Two of them were brothers and the third was a childhood friend. They told the story of how they worked all winter saving money only to leave it all behind and hitch hike into the great northwest with no real destination or goal. They seemed to be happy just being together, enjoying nature and reading their Bibles.

After some cordial conversation, one of them finally asked the question that would change everything.

"So, did y'all make it to the bus?"

"No dude, the river was too swift, we couldn't cross. So, we're just gonna chill for a bit and head on back toward the car."

"Oh, well, we were just there, yesterday, we can show you where to cross."

Ummm, exqueeze me? Baking powder? Did you goof balls just say you made it to the bus in jeans and flannel? What the heck, man? What were we missing? How the…? What the…? Where the…? Did I just write an entire paragraph of nothing but questions? Maybe.

We must have looked like school kids sitting in a circle listening to the teacher read us a story before naptime, a captive audience to say the least. The hippies went on to describe how they made it across the river and hiked to the bus. They were curious about this whole bus thing, so just for shits and giggles they tried to cross the river. They didn't want to get all their clothes wet, so they full up crossed the river in board shorts and bare feet, holding their flip flops over their heads. When they reached the far bank they realized their mistake of not having proper hiking shoes for the remaining ten miles to the bus, so they came back across the river barefoot in board shorts. They packed up small packs with shorts and hiking boots and crossed the river a third time, barefoot and in board shorts.

Hearing this made me sick. How in the world could these kids conquer this river barefooted and in board shorts, and we couldn't seem to figure it out? They certainly had my attention now. We asked them specifics and eventually they offered to show us where they crossed and give us a tutorial on getting to the bus from there. As if we had no time to spare, we hastily threw our junk back in our packs and chased the hippies south toward their camp. We never even lit the cigars.

✦

Smokus and I got a wild hair one February Saturday morning while deployed to Kunsan, South Korea. Boredom had already taken its toll in just the first few weeks of this deployment, so we decided to grab a car and head out into the country and find a hill to climb. Two others joined in with us, so the four of us loaded up and took off with no real destination, at first. Eventually, we settled on driving a couple of hours to a popular hiking trail in Deogyusan National Park, in the center of the peninsula. Doing our best to interpret the road signs and get through populated areas without sticking out too much or killing someone, we finally made it to the parking lot for the trailhead.

Snow had fallen several days during our short stay in the country this far, but this day was a bright, clear, sunny day with no wind. The sky was deep blue behind the snow-covered mountains below, with only a few puffy white clouds dotting here and there. After gearing up and heading up the trail awhile, we noticed the path getting more and more icy as we climbed higher in elevation. Trees covered the trail, so very little sunlight made it to the ground, preventing the snow and ice from melting. The going was slow but steady, when a large Korean man coming down the opposite direction stopped and stared at us.

Laughing bold belly laughs in a booming Korean voice and bouncing around us like a Korean version of the Kool-Aid man, he yelled, "Ha, ha, ha! You no make it. You no have Crampons! Ha, ha, ha!"

Oh. No. He. Didn't. Now, hold up a second. If I had to name three outdoor activities the South Koreans really put money into, they would be golf, skiing, and hiking. But this dude was legit probably 300 pounds plus. That said, he was decked to the gills with the best, most expensive name brand hiking gear. From his Mountain Hardware beanie, to his Keen hiking boots, and all The North Face and Marmot in between, he certainly looked the part. Rounding out his high-priced outfit were his stupid Crampons, the slip on, ice-spike attachments to his over-priced hiking boots. He was clearly a better outdoorsman than either of us.

Fueled by the motivation of a never-quit attitude and dressed in our finest military-issued cold weather clothes, we slipped and slid all the way to the top. Ok, our fuel was more rage at the Korean Kool-Aid guy for saying we couldn't do it. Reaching the top, we touched the summit and got our pictures taken by a friendly Korean-American family before heading back down.

Like our hike to the bus, Smokus and I had been arguably unprepared for the exact conditions of this trail but continued upward and ended with a successful summit. Smokus and I being unprepared for a hike seems to be a trend, I guess, huh? Also, just like our bus hike, one of our buddies began the hike in military-issued, black, steel-toed Bellville combat boots causing him to slip and fall every other step on the way down. Thankfully, Smokus had brought a pair of sneakers and loaned them to the guy for the walk down the mountain. Had he not done this, the guy would have surely slipped and landed in a pile at the bottom. Maybe the large Korean dude would have broken his fall.

So, what's the moral of the story, boys? Well, just like calling Marty McFly a chicken, nobody, but nobody tells me I can't do something, especially, the over-weight, over-geared, Korean Stay-Puff-Marshmallow man. What one man can do, so can another. If these damn hippies can ford this river barefooted, well, by God...

Following the same Kunsan, South Korea deployment, where we hiked with no Crampons, a small detachment of our squadron stopped at Joint Base Pearl Harbor, Hawaii for a couple of weeks on the return trip back to Idaho. We'd just spent four months in the grips of the South Korean winter, so Hawaii was a welcome reprieve from freezing cold temperatures and barren landscapes. We all welcomed the warm, thick, humid air and bright sunshine, but could have done without the daily afternoon thunderstorms. After a few days of getting sunburned next to the pool, drinking Mai Tais, it was time to see the countryside of Oahu.

We got some gouge from the locals on some easy hikes, doable in an afternoon. One guy recommended a specific short hike close by, so we socialized the idea around the group, and three of us decided to attempt to make it to a waterfall in the Hawaiian jungle, late one afternoon. The directions to the waterfall were simple enough: follow the highway to exit whatever, go into the neighborhood, bear right at some point and park at the end of the street next to the house with the loud dog. Follow the trail from there and you'll find it no problem. Uh, ok.

No kidding, the directions were spot on. We had no problems finding the trailhead, but soon after departing from the car we were getting drenched in the routine afternoon monsoons. Hiking in swimming trunks and regular walking shoes, we scurried through the mud slipping and falling a couple of billion times along the way. The waterfall was only two miles back and we made good time, despite the weather.

Following a short scramble up a narrow path of a flowing creek, rocks and exposed tree roots, we were staring at the waterfall. Honestly, we didn't initially see what all the fuss was about. The pool at the bottom was only about 20 feet across and who knows how deep, but the creek and falls were only about seven or eight feet above the top of the small pool. This is not exactly what I had in mind when the dude said it was fun to jump off the rocks into the pool. I thought it was kind of weak sauce to be completely honest. Suddenly, appearing out of nowhere, a young man looking to be in his late teens scampered up the trail.

The young man looked like the stereotypical Hawaiian surfer dude with his wavy, dark brown hair flopping about his head as he root-hopped up the trail to the bank of the pool. Barefooted, shirtless and in swim trunks, he didn't speak to us at all, nor did he hesitate to jump into the freezing cold waters of the pool and climb up the falls on the left side. After crossing the shallow creek above the falls to the right side, the young dude climbed like he was half mountain goat and half American Ninja Warrior to a small outcropping overlooking the pool 30 feet below. Without warning or announcement, the Hawaiian spider monkey jumped out and did a magnificent cannonball into the small pool. Cowabunga, dude! I give you a 10.

Apparently satisfied with his accomplishments, the young man lazily swam to the pool's edge and climbed out next to us where we stood staring in disbelief. I guess we had this "What the hell?" look on our faces, so he proceeded to tell us exactly how to go and what to look for to get to the ledge he had jumped from. He also reminded us not to pee in the pool or else the tiny-microscopic-bug-fish-parasite thingy will swim up our wiener holes and lodge itself in. Whoa! Huh? No thank you. The official name of the tiny parasitic freshwater catfish he was warning about is the Candiru, or *Vandellia cirrhosa*. A tropical fish, it is also known in Amazonian lore as the Vampire Catfish, and not native to Hawaii. Yeah, um, I don't know about this, man.

Blood sucking wiener-loving catfish be damned, I jumped in and swam across the pool, straining not to pee the entire way. Following the short scramble up the rock on the far side I made it to the ledge, squatted a few seconds and jumped for it. That was awesome! I was also not interested in doing it again for fear of the little vampire fish do-dad. Here's the point of the whole story: A) don't be afraid to try something new, and B) sometimes you have to just go for it regardless of your fears or phobias. You might just enjoy it and forever be able to say, "Yeah, I've jumped off a waterfall in Hawaii, and I didn't get a catfish stuck in my dick hole."

✦

The six of us approached the hippie camp and took a wide berth on some higher ground through the alder thicket and emerged on the bank in the same spot where Banzai and I had concluded there was no way someone crossed there. The current was simply too swift. Standing on the shore, the hippies educated us on the laws of hydrodynamics as applied in Alaskan river system. The small alder we had seen taking a beating in the current was actually fighting back a little. The tiny bush may have looked like a leaved version of a wacky-wavy-inflatable-flailing-arm-tube man in front of a used car dealership, but on the downstream side of the alder, the current was broken and not nearly as strong. The hippies told us to get to that point and orient ourselves a little more upstream, then step off into the main current. As described before, the main current was only a couple of feet wide, but the way it swirled around that tattered alder made the eddies push toward the far bank. If we could get to that point, the eddies would swirl us and push us right into the bank on the opposite side. I have to admit, it was pretty smart and I didn't think of it. Geniuses in flannel. Well done, hippies, well done.

Of course, I got to be the guinea pig for this little episode. After making plans with Smokus and Banzai that if this didn't work, they would notify my next of kin and tell my kids I died a hero, I made sure my pockets were empty, got my pack on just right and plopped down into the current. There was no easing my way in. I immediately stood in water rushing very fast and up to my thighs. Using my stick, I braced against the current and headed for the alder with five dry cheerleaders behind me on the bank. Reaching the area where the alder broke the current really wasn't too bad, but I knew the worst was yet to come. Standing there behind the small bush, I made up my mind and took a step toward the far shore, immediately stepping into the current and water up to my belt. I supposed the adrenaline and anxiety of the situation masked the fact that once more my balls were submerged in freezing cold glacier water. Just as the hippies predicted, the current swirled and pushed me a few feet downstream and spit me out, right into the far bank.

I grabbed a small tree and climbed out, wet and cold but no worse for wear. I don't know if they secretly hoped I would lose footing and disappear into the Alaskan interior or if they were excited for my success, but Smokus and Banzai followed one after the other. Standing on opposite sides of the river we bid the hippies adieu and walked to the west side of the island. We still had to cross the bigger, wider part of the river, but according to the hippies we had really done the worst part, and it was relatively smooth sailing from here on.

The wide portion of the crossing wasn't too bad at all. I led with Smokus and Banzai in trail, and in no time we were standing on dry ground on the west side of the Tek. Before Smokus and Banzai even got out of the water I had my camera out and recorded the moment.

"Video diary continued! All that bullshit that Banzai just said a while ago, we just met some crusty hippies that showed us how to cross the fucking river, and here we are across the mighty Tek, we're going to the bus!"

Slowly dripping dry on the water's edge of the Tek, Banzai, Smokus, and I were far from Hawaii, but we had done something awesome, at least in our own minds. We'd beaten our nemesis. We'd won. It didn't take us long to realize we still had a long way to go.

FLYING VAMPIRES

O N THE WEST shore of the Teklanika River we rested for a few minutes. Exhausted from the physical and emotional toll the previous two hours had taken, we needed a little time to digest the gravity of what just transpired. Individually, we had each accepted the fact our goal of reaching the Bus was significantly out of reach. Admitting to ourselves that crushing defeat was one of the lowest lows, but that singular emotion pivoted to the equally opposite direction when the hippies emerged from wherever the hell they came from. Manifest from the heavens, or out of a deep slumber in that blue tent, who knows? Either way, they changed our mood and our reality. Now, standing on the western shore of that formidable obstacle, we were simultaneously elated and anxious.

The Tek marked the halfwayish point on the journey. So, for anyone who's counting, we had completed roughly one fourth of our entire trip. When the government takes twenty-five percent of your money for taxes it's a big deal, and you think twenty-five is way too much. When you have completed only twenty-five percent of a physical and emotional roller coaster, you realize that one fourth is really not that much—ten of forty miles. One fourth. Twenty-five percent. Holy shit, we have a long way to go man. I was cold, achy, tired, hungry, and I smelled like football locker room, but the thought of getting to the Bus had once more become reality, so we prepared for the next phase.

At one point in my life, I became obsessed with long distance hikes. I have watched countless hours of documentary footage from people who have thru-hiked the Appalachian Trail, Pacific Crest Trail and the Continental Divide Trail. The scenery is nothing short of spectacular and the trips are all epic. While all three trails offer a slightly different experience, they all share several common themes.

For starters, all three trails are over 2100 miles long. The Appalachian Trail (AT) is the shortest measuring a puny 2190 miles according to the Appalachian Trail Conservatory, but it also has the most overall elevation gain of the three. The Pacific Crest Trail (PCT) is longer at 2650 miles, and the Continental Divide Trail (CDT) is the longest and most rugged at 3100 miles. Each trail takes roughly six months to complete start to finish.

The single most prevalent aspect of hiking any one of these trails is the will and determination it takes to complete. Every documentary of a successful thru hike highlights the same theme: high energy at the start, invariably a point in the middle where doubt creeps in, and ultimately a jubilant finish. The routine of hiking, eating, sleeping, pooping, cooking, setting up and tearing down camp, eventually takes its toll on even the most determined and motivated hikers. A well-documented phenomenon of the human anatomy is the idea that the mind will give up long before the body physically does, and that weakening of the spirit is what ultimately overtakes many hikers and forces them to quit.

The idea of setting out on a 3000-mile hike is daunting. Planning is long and intense and must account for more variables than you can list. The size and scope of a thru-hike on one of these trails is unimaginable, and a hiker must put it all in a backpack to carry all provisions for every obstacle. There is no way a person could carry enough equipment or food to account for everything. Not only would the equipment be way too heavy, but each of these trails traverses varying ecosystems, each requiring a different set of equipment and skills. Detailed and robust planning is a key to success on any trail.

Another well-documented aspect of these "super hikes" is the gear shakedowns where hikers ditch gear they realize they either don't need or isn't practical to carry for 2000 plus miles. Discarded items are as simple as coffee mugs to axes to full size pillows to multiple wardrobes to extra "fill-in-the-blank". When you carry your whole world on your back and climb a 14,000-foot mountain, suddenly you re-evaluate what really matters and is important.

Our bus journey was not a "super hike" by any stretch of the imagination. Our hike would barely register as an interesting day to anyone who has completed, or even attempted, one of the American Triple Crown thru hikes. Our trip was wimpy by comparison. Any AT thru hiker would tell tales of many river crossings, mountain climbs, bugs, snakes, bears, boredom, achy feet, monotony, hunger, and melancholy. Our trip does not hold water when compared to these epics. Our trip wasn't even particularly pretty or exciting. Out trip was rather boring. Our trip was…our trip, special and significant only to us.

Looking back at the river, we gathered our composure and turned west. Soggy, waterlogged and cold, we stepped ahead once more toward the bus. Banzai had been alternating between his Asics running shoes and Danner military issued combat boots. The sneakers were immeasurably more comfortable, but they offered little in protection from elements and terrain. The boots on the other hand, kept his feet safe from the rocks and cold water to some degree, but weighed 300 pounds (estimated) when soaked and covered in Alaskan mud and muck. This would be his conundrum for the entire trip. Smokus and I both, at least, wore proper hiking shoes. Though they were equally water logged, they were still at least more comfortable than desert tan military combat boots.

Even outfitted with good shoes, ten miles is a thing. I'd challenge anyone to put on their best shoes and walk ten miles. Flat, hilly, muddy, sandy, paved. Doesn't matter. Ten miles is a long distance no matter how you shake it. Maybe it's not even the sore feet, but the monotony that ends up getting in the mind and playing games. Regardless, every step was torture for each of us for various reasons. To compare each other's personal plight would be like measuring happiness. It meant something different to all of us, and only he knew whether or not he could push through.

Setting out from the river, we approached another series of beaver ponds. These ponds had been blown up with dynamite in the past, but on our day, they were intact and created several deep ponds. We'd sort of had it with water at this point, and luckily the trail supported us by spanning around or over the beaver dams, keeping us more or less dry. Crossing this set of beaver ponds did not conjure the soprano wails the eastern ponds managed. In fact, I'm not sure we even got our feet wet, let alone our nether regions.

Almost immediately after crossing the ponds, we climbed to higher ground as the trail wound westward up a small hill. The higher trail was now a proper double track road fit for a small SUV or four-wheeler ATV. The trail was not nearly as wet as the previous sections, but overgrown with vegetation pressing in from the sides. The new section was rather smooth and undulating as it traversed hill after hill through the green tunnel of trees and brush. Drying out after a short time, it suddenly hit us that we were now hiking in prime grizzly country, and in the early Alaskan afternoon the sun came out and with it the ambient temperature rose. In other words, we were sweating our asses off, both from the threat of becoming lunch to North America's largest predator and the stifling heat. But then there was something else totally unpredicted.

When I first moved to Alaska in November 2000, the air was cold, and the ground was covered in its snowy white blanket that would last until April. In April and May we experienced what was known as "break-up", aptly named due to the snow and ice melting away for the last time until around September. The end of May brought warm sunny days, cool nights and mosquitoes. I had heard tales of the mosquitoes, but I'd also grown up in the south where mosquitoes are everywhere. That summer of 2001, I gained a new appreciation for that winged, blood-sucking insect. Anyone who has ever visited Alaska will know what I mean when I say the state bird of Alaska is the mosquito.

The mosquitoes in Alaska are cut from a different cloth than any I had previously encountered. These things were like ravenous, winged vampires that could get through anything. They would get through car doors, house walls, and clothing like it wasn't even there. I still think their barbed snout bloodsucker thingy (formally known as the "proboscis") was like a six-inch hypodermic needle made of titanium. Bug spray that contained anything less than 30 percent DEET (N, N-diethyl-meta-toluamide) just made Alaskan mosquitoes high and want to attack in swarms like World War II fighter jets on bombing runs over Germany.

✦

In 21 years of active military service, I had only been told once to go home, pack a bag, and be ready to deploy in 24 hours. It was June in Alaska, so when we got the notification, we were all pissed off at the idea of having to leave the State during one of the best months all year. Why do we have to deploy to some shit hole, for God knows how long, while literally every species of salmon is filling the rivers? This was also in the time before smart phones and text messages, so the only way to get information was to call the other dude and play the telephone game. As the day wore on, the bro network revealed our destination: King Salmon, Alaska.

King Salmon is a small town near the western coast of Alaska. The only way to get there is to fly in or boat up the river from the Bering Sea. June...Alaska...King Salmon. Our packing list immediately changed. Out came all the cold weather gear and in went all the fishing gear. Imagine 10 dudes sitting in the back of a C-130 with their bags between their legs, fishing poles sticking up out of each. We looked a lot more like a fishing expedition than a forward deployment of troops.

The first day we were there we actually had some work to do getting our F-15s bedded down in the shelters. When we completed the care and feeding of the jets, we all set out for a short two- or three-mile hike to the nearest fishing stream. Today's goal: Rainbow Trout. We slipped down the bank and into the water, fishing flies going everywhere. As we fished, we eased our way down stream, rounded a bend and entered an area with steep walls and cliff-like edges. The scenery was serene, the fishing was alright, and the brotherhood was awesome. Continuing downstream for a couple of hundred yards, the banks leveled out to reveal meadows and open grass and brush on either side. That's when they attacked.

If I were to plan an attack, I would have done it the same way. Like something from a Jason Bourne movie, lure the unsuspecting travelers into an inescapable position and distract them with a scenic diversion. Then, suddenly and viciously attack. Give no quarter. Leave nothing but rotting corpses. No survivors. Dead men tell no tales. The mosquitoes had clearly studied General Norman Schwarzkopf's "shock and awe" strategy that won the first Gulf War in just 42 days. In swarms and formations that blotted out the sun, like the arrow attack in the movie 300, the mosquitoes ambushed us in that narrow stream. With no downstream exit available, we were forced to return back the direction we came. The mosquitoes apparently expected this move and set up a blockade along the way. I'm convinced they communicated telepathically or telekinetically to choreograph that assault on us peaceful fishermen. I had sprayed myself completely with Off bug spray with 30 percent DEET, but the mosquitoes seemed unphased by my repellant. In fact, they appeared to get high on it or something, propelling them like crystal meth tweakers in a race from the cops. I would have been better off if I had bathed myself in meat juice and run into the bear den at the zoo. I was precariously positioned with no defenses. Retreating as quickly as I could against the current of the stream and knowing it could be my last tactical glove save, I removed my hat, drenched it and my cranium in DEET a second time, and waved my hat in front of my face to prevent the kamikaze vampire insects from entering through my mouth. Eventually we made it back, weak from blood loss, and each of us certainly infected with some blood-born parasite or virus that would be the end of humankind. I was patient zero.

✦

And so it went on the Stampede Trail. The once frozen permafrost had melted into a juicy petri dish quagmire providing a perfect laboratory for Mother Nature to grow the Alaska state bird. Clouds retreated to the distances and the summer sun beat down on us hard. Once soaking wet and frozen by a glacial river, we now tried to remove as much clothing as possible to beat the heat, high and dry with little water and right through prime grizzly country. I guess now would be a good time to mention we had no gun or bear spray. All we had was a 99-cent bear bell I wore on my pack, and I'm pretty sure it didn't even work. Our sole defense against the great Alaskan grizzly bear was talking loudly. I reckon you can imagine how little conversation we were actively having given our physical and mental states.

I'm confident the mosquitoes had been following us for miles waiting for that perfect time and place to launch their aerial assault. In and out of the green tunnel of the trail we walked, progressively losing clothes to the scorch of the heat. Morale and water rations were low, grizzly awareness was high. Then, out of nowhere they attacked. Like stealth fighters using radar and GPS, they swarmed and contained us. We had no escape and no recourse. We were caught in a conundrum. We could put clothes back on and sweat to death, or we could continue presently meeting death with a million bites. Of course, maybe the mosquitoes would be messy eaters, leave traces of blood everywhere and leave us to be a salty, sweaty dinner for the grizz. Would we bleed out or become lunch? When faced with impossible decisions, you must keep your wits and persevere. This is easier said than done.

I, for one, was running out of gas quickly. I used most of my cognitive, emotional and physical equity crossing that river. I was to the point of encouraging myself, cheering on "left foot, right foot." Smokus fared no better. He reported seeing stop signs in the trail as he begrudgingly trekked westward. "Hey, did you guys hear that music?" was a common conversation by this point. There's no music, Banzai, just the buzz of mosquitoes planning the next ambush, the sounds of us slapping ourselves repeatedly in vain to kill the little bastards, and the crunch of our tired feet on the trail. Banzai had been hallucinating for a while, and eventually gave into his delusions and had conversations with an imaginary Bigfoot that was paralleling us through the woods, or so he claimed. Even with losing our individual battles with reality and desire to continue, we strode on. The only sounds were the occasional rustle of leaves, the rhythmic crunch of our footsteps on the trail, and the repeating "THWACK!" of another mosquito meeting his maker by the hands of its prey. Dying a little with each step and mosquito bite, we kept pace toward the bus.

I did not take many pictures on this portion of the trail. Defeating delirium and fatigue was almost my sole focus, so we stopped periodically to hydrate and rest our worn feet and gather ourselves, each trying to give a pep talk to the other. The scene in Talladega nights where Ricky Bobby is trying to psych himself up to get in the car with the cougar, Karen, comes to mind. "Awe man, Aaaaawwww, I'm just gonna do it, I'm gonna do it right now. I'm gonna get in that car and drive it. AAAAHHHH SHIT, it's a cougar!"

Banzai took advantage of these rest periods to get the camera out and film me checking the GPS to see how far we had gone. The answers were never reassuring; rather, each check of the distance was slightly more demoralizing than the previous. I guess we all hoped that we would all of a sudden check the GPS and it would simply say, "You're there, man!". Banzai, panning the camera from left to right mostly focusing on his face in Blair Witch Project fashion, updated and marked an occasional rest stop. His voice was flat, void of emotions, and he gazed into the camera with the most devastating resting bitch face (RBF) ever captured on camera.

> "Alright, we're at the 33-hour point. Roscoe, Smokus over there. I think I speak for everyone right now when I say life is, simply put, misery. Umm, everything hurts. I'm tired. I've seen delusions of Bigfoot. So, I think we're almost there. Roscoe's getting ready for a distance update, so hopefully at the next hour check in we'll be there, but only God knows."

Each time we checked the distance was a slap-in-the-face reminder of how far we had remaining, which always seemed to send our morale farther down. The 33-hour point he referenced was our elapsed time awake, based on an 0600 wake up on Friday morning. Though we had walked for what seemed like hours, we still had miles to go. The best description of relativity I've heard is in the movie Deep Blue Sea. LL Cool J's character explains relatively: "Grab hold of a hot pan and a second can seem like an hour. Put your hands on a hot woman and an hour seems like a second." For us, Einstein's theory of relativity was in full effect.

In the distance we noticed the light, fluffy, white clouds were darkening as the afternoon heat grew. Thermal heating was beginning to raise the low, heavy humid air higher into the atmosphere forming the infant stages of a series of cumulonimbus clouds, a prelude to a potentially thunderous afternoon. Watching closely, we were sure the worst of the weather would remain south of us closer to the Alaska Range, but with any luck, remain close enough to provide us with welcome shade for the remaining daylight hours. Our final rest stop along the trail was anticlimactic, despite the fact that GPS said we had only a half-mile to go. We were so tired I guess it didn't even register. I mean, the stupid thing didn't say, "Dude, you're there!" so we turned it off and stored it, drank some water and geared up.

With my eyes focused on the trail six feet in front I almost didn't even see the smoke rising ahead. The faint column of dark smoke rose just ahead, but walking through the green tunnel of the trail did not allow for a good view of the clearing until we stepped into it. Without warning or thundering applause or confetti, there it was. I took us 14 hours, but we had reached Fairbanks city bus 142—The Magic Bus.

THE BUS

63° 52' 6.24" N, 149° 46' 9.48" W

THE CLEARING IN the trail was relatively small, measuring only 15 yards across and 20 long, or so. To the left of the trail, next to the edge of the woods, near a short cliff overlooking the Sushana River, sat the broken-down hulk of the 1946 K5 International Harvester, Fairbanks Bus 142. Covered primarily in a faded white and green shell with hints of yellow peeking through at the seams where the paint was weathered away, the bus just sat there without applause or grandeur. Quiet and still, with flat tires, bullet holes and broken glass, the bus looked dilapidated and worn down. In the foreground next to a small makeshift fire ring was a man sitting in a broken chair drying his wrinkled feet and drenched clothing. Surprised, we introduced ourselves as we approached.

Hendrick was a German hiker who had bushwhacked around 20 miles north from Denali National Park along the Sushana River reaching the bus only a short while before we arrived. He had planned to backpack through Denali when somehow he caught wind of "this bus thing," and decided to come see what all the fuss was about. He said he had just set up his tent, gathered up some wood and started a fire, when out of nowhere we popped out of the wilderness. We hadn't predicted or even considered the idea that someone else would share our Magic Bus experience, and I'm sure we looked like the RCA dog with his head cocked to the side in bewilderment as we stood there trying to take it all in.

There was no finish line. No ribbon to run through. No table with volunteers handing out fruit like there would be if we finished a marathon. No medals. No applause or congratulations. Aside from our heavy breathing and small talk with Hendrick, there was only silence and stillness. It was very peaceful. Looking back, I can imagine what it was like for McCandless to stay there for 114 days without seeing another person. Just him and the breeze. It must have been sublime.

Hendrick was just as exhausted as we were, and the entire time we explored the site and sat with him, he never moved from the chair. He told his tale of getting off the bus in Denali National Park and turning north following the Sushana River. His trail quickly disappeared, and he found himself getting beaten by the dense alder thickets along the shore. With nothing but the river as his guide, he bushwhacked around 20 miles to get to his present location. No wonder he didn't want to stand. Our walk had been tiresome, but at least we were on a trail of sorts. Hendrick had worked hard for a long time and he earned his rest.

We snapped out of our daze, laughed at Hendrick's joke about selling postcards of the Bus, removed our gear and began to take it all in. The surrounding area is not all that spectacular, just a clearing off the side of the trail. The foliage didn't change at all. The Bus sits on high ground just a few yards from the Sushana River. Without the burden of our packs we explored the Bus.

Opening the door and climbing up the steps, we caught our first glimpse inside. It was exactly how my mind projected it based on the pictures I'd seen and from the book and movie. A metal-framed foldable chair sat where normally would be the driver's seat, but the steering wheel remained. Turing left and standing at the front of the Bus, the interior was rusted and dirty, but picked up and not extremely cluttered. The bus looked not comfortable, but cozy. Immediately we could see the allure of wanting to make a stay here. It really did have potential for a good backcountry camp, especially for a dude without sustainable shelter of any kind.

Next to the left wall sat a small shelf containing various items and goods left by passersby and campers. Remember the "take one, leave one" stuff? This was it. Notably, there was a bottle of bear spray and a jar of rice, presumably homage to McCandless in a small way. When he departed from his ride at the head of the Stampede Trail, he carried a bag of rice for sustenance. Beyond the shelf was a barrel-shaped wood burning stove and heater, the six-inch smokestack rising through the ceiling. In the rear of the Bus, perpendicular to the length and sitting atop a metal frame to keep it off the floor, was the remains of a deteriorated mattress. Most of the fabric had wasted away revealing its rusted springs. We surmised this was the very mattress on which Chris McCandless was found dead in his sleeping bag. On the right-hand side of the bus were a few shelves housing suitcases filled with notebooks and journals for hikers to sign and write vigils to McCandless. In the case containing the notebooks we found a note to hikers. Written by hand on a notebook sheet of paper and wrapped in a worn and weathered Ziploc bag was a handwritten note to visitors to the Bus that read:

> No matter what you think of the man who spent 4 months here in 1992, please do the following to help keep this shelter clean:
>> 1. Remove all trash from the stove before you depart.
>> 2. Stock extra kindling and logs inside for the next visitor.
>> 3. Sweep the floor.
>> 4. Pack out one supply item that is no longer good. Leave a new item if you wish.
>> 5. Respect, don't degrade this shelter/memorial.
>> Leave all McCandless items neatly in place.
>
> Thank you.

The walls of the bus were scribed with signatures, short poems, motivational quotes, and inspirations written by previous hikers. The McCandless family had visited the Bus not long after learning of their son's demise. In addition to, and standing out from the graffiti written in marker, the family attached a brass plaque that reads:

CHRISTOPHER JOHNSON MCCANDLESS

"ALEX"

2/69 - 8/92

CHRIS, OUR BELOVED SON AND BROTHER DIED HERE DURING HIS ADVENTUROUS TRAVELS IN SEARCH OF HOW HE COULD BEST REALIZE GOD'S GREAT GIFT OF LIFE. WITH HIS FINAL MESSAGE, "I HAVE HAD A HAPPY LIFE AND THANK THE LORD, GOODBYE AND MAY GOD BLESS ALL", WE COMMEND HIS SOUL TO THE WORLD.

THE MCCANDLESS FAMILY, 7/93

We only spent a few minutes inside the Bus, but the event was a bit surreal. Not emotionally moving, but familiar. I knew the story well, but seeing it with my own eyes brought it to life even more vividly than reading any book or watching any movie could. I'm not saying I was profoundly touched or had a moment or anything, but the experience resonated, and I was proud to have gotten to see it. After taking a few pictures and videos to commemorate our achievement (as well as render proof to our doubters), we signed the ledgers, stuck our Squadron patch on the door, and signed the wall around it with a Sharpie. We exited the Bus and took a few more pictures sitting on and around the exterior before finally stripping down and sitting with Hendrick by his fire.

Hendrick traded me some coffee for a small baggie of Cheez-its I had bought from the convenience store on the Air Force Base a few days prior. We told our story of the hippies and sat there for about 30 minutes drying our clothes and shoes and resting. In the distance, the rumbling of thunder grew louder and closer, warning us once more how precarious our situation really was, and that we were running close on time to make it back. Smokus, Banzai and I walked down to the Sushana River one last time, took in the views and refilled our water bottles. The river valley was tranquil and beautiful with the Sushana babbling quietly over small river rocks and winding away to the west before disappearing into the wilderness. Again, I couldn't help but think how awesome McCandless must have felt about his situation living in the Bus. We filled our water containers, returned to Hendrick still sitting by his fire, and prepared for the return trip to our car 20-something miles east. We left Hendrick to his own solitude and marched off down the trail at around 1830 Saturday evening. After all the sweat and toil to get there, we stayed at the Bus less than an hour, and never smoked the cigars.

GRANITE TORS

ARRIVAL IN ALASKA meant the beginning of a three-week deployment built around flying combat-like sorties with hundreds of other aircraft. Landing at Eielson AFB, AK would have been exciting if it weren't for the hours and hours of briefings we were forced to endure prior to getting set in our rooms for the evening and rest of the trip. While sitting in these briefings we made friends with some of the locals at the Base and began to pry out intel on the good hiking and fishing spots in the local surrounding area. One friendly local we met recommended the Granite Tors trail, just north of Fairbanks off Chena Hot Springs Road. The trail was reported to be only about a five-mile loop and relatively easy. With the day complete we summoned the posse and set out around 1900 for the trailhead.

The parking lot at the trailhead was situated right on the Chena River across Chena Hot Springs Road from the actual trail. Our group of about 10 bailed out of our rental cars and geared up for the hike. The forest across the road looked thick and beautiful, building anticipation of our late evening hike. As I looked around the group, I started to notice a very eclectic mix of preparation and gear. Some like me wore proper hiking shoes and shorts, carried back packs, and at least looked the part. Others wore pants and sneakers with no packs at all. One ole chap wore Carhartt twill pants and running shoes. One thing that really stood out to me was the lack of water some brought. I had a small Camelback bladder in my pack and by far carried the most water of the group. A few had Nalgene bottles full, but some simply carried a one-liter bottle from the convenience store. Foreshadowing, maybe?

Departing the parking lot, we made our way to the trail and soon the group fanned out, each getting comfortable with his own pace. We ran into a fellow hiker coming down the East Trail as we headed out. He explained how the trail was a loop comprised of the East Trail and the West Trail. The East trail, while a little longer, was a more gradual incline overall and provided an easier path to the Tors with mostly boardwalk covering the boggy marsh below. The West Trail was through a boggy marsh and contained a portion that was almost straight up. The hiker, a local, let us know most people go out on the East Trail and return via the West Trail due to the steep terrain. Our group quickly voted and determined that we would continue on the preferred East Trail route, so we started to march on. At this point the hiker let us in on a key piece of knowledge we could have used about an hour ago while gearing up: the loop was 14 miles long. Depending on the source, the trail is rated as moderate, strenuous and difficult, and 14 miles is a long hike even for a well-prepared outdoorsman, let alone someone in jeans and just one bottle of water.

With the sun still up in the late evening, the air temperature was warm enough to have us sweating almost immediately. Huffing and puffing as we made our way through the forest and up the incline, the trees of the forest began to thin out, giving way to direct sunlight for a large portion of the hike. We walked for a significant distance through a portion of forest that had burned in 2004, which not only made us hotter due to a lack of shade, but stirred up clouds of ashy dust as our herd marched through. The surrounding terrain was arid and dry, hot and steep.

Several miles into the loop, the trail plateaued into an alpine meadow leading to the backcountry shelter labeled on the trail map we glanced at in the parking lot. The shelter is situated on flat, high ground and within closing distance to the Tors, but the surrounding tundra was soggy and muddy all around. The peat moss had mixed with the rain, permafrost and moisture to create a bog that again would swallow shoes of not tied on tight. We rested at the shelter for what seemed like a long time, allowing the dude in Carhartts to roll up his pants and take his shoes off. When we finally decided to get back to the hike, many of our party reported they were out of water already. We still had many, many miles to go and the sun was not getting any cooler.

The gang departed the shelter and headed toward our destination. Those who had worn only sneakers carried them in their hands in order to not get them covered in Alaskan backcountry muck. Thirsty and sweaty, we forged on reaching the "Plain of Monuments" containing the Granite Tors, soon after leaving the shelter.

The Granite Tors are a series of granite spires shooting

up from the ground, looming high above the alpine tundra. Millions of years ago, lava and molten rock flowed up from deep inside the earth but cooled prior to breaching the surface. Millennia of erosion eventually revealed the towering spires majestically dotting the horizon. The Tors are now an attraction and a popular destination for hikers, campers, photographers, and painters.

We climbed several of the rock formations, took lots of pictures, and ate snacks. Well, at least a few of us did. As I sat on a spire alone enjoying the vista, I retrieved a plain cheeseburger I had kept from the chow hall prior to leaving the Base. Some of my fellow outdoorsmen watched my every move like my black Labrador Retriever, Tucker, watching my wife eat pizza. He knows if he is patient and puts on his best pouty face, she will give him the crust. I quickly understood what was going on. Nobody brought snacks for the trip. No water. No snacks. No shoes. What the fuck were these dudes thinking? Then again, who am I to judge, right?

At any rate, we sat for a while, folks watched others eat, and we collectively decided it was time to get on back to the car. Sticking with the original plan to take the West Trail, we climbed the rock outcropping on the trail toward the forest. The trail steepened and ducked in and out of spruce and alder thickets, but at least we were heading down this time. Several of our group, were now gulping water from my Camelback at every stop, their water having given out miles ago. Twisting and turning through the forest, we made it to a ledge where the trail seemed to go straight down. Slipping and falling down the loose rock covering the trail, we landed at the bottom in a cloud of dust, mouths dry and eyes watering.

The trail was well maintained for most of the entire route, with the minor exception of the area surrounding the Tors where the trail kind of disappeared into more of a "chose your own adventure" type feeling. This last portion of the West Trail was a boardwalk built over a swampy series of ponds and marsh. Thirst had taken its toll on many of the group, and now with at least a decent water source, they took my offer of Iodine tablets to add to their bottles, and scoop up some of the dirty pond water.

Anyone who has never used Iodine tabs before should know a couple of things. First, you are supposed to wait 30 minutes before drinking the now purified water. Second, it tastes like shit! When you've been that thirsty for that long I guess it doesn't matter. A few of the guys didn't even wait the required time limit and chugged the water down as fast as they could. I continued down the trail to the car, kicked off my shoes and rested my tired feet in the freezing cold Chena River. Several hours after departure, and exhausted from the hot dusty trail, one by one the remaining stragglers made their way to the car and we returned back to the Base.

So what's the moral of the story? You see, kids, even grown men are knuckleheads from time to time. Take this away from this debacle: prepare every hike as if it is a long, dry, hot, cold, wet mess. Carry water and a fire starter. Wear proper clothes. All of these elementary little things can be the difference in a great experience and getting into real trouble. Our group did not provide a good example. No new lessons, just lessons re-learned. If only I would take my own advice.

REVERSE

EVERYTHING WE HAD encountered up to this point was the direct result of a decision we made. At any time, we could have chosen differently to yield a different outcome or circumstance. The fact that we had 20 miles, two rivers, hippies, beaver ponds, mud and water to traverse to get back to our car only to endure a three-hour road trip was 100 percent on us. Decisions we make in our day-to-day lives produce consequences. Some are good and some are not so good. The constant with them all, is the root cause. When something happens with my kids, I ask them every time "Who did this to you?" The answer is almost always "You did this to you". Our current position was no different. We had gotten us into this mess and now we had no choice in the matter. Getting our feet wet in the beginning, post-holing through mud, crossing the rivers, it all led us to this moment. Getting to the bus was fun and exciting. Going back was non-negotiable and daunting. We were now forced to go back through everything. Heading out to the Bus was like drinking and partying on Saturday night. This walk back was going to be the inevitable hangover Sunday morning.

Hendrick sat idly in the same spot as when we arrived an hour before, staring blankly into his small fire still warming and drying his feet and clothes. As we shook hands and bid farewell, we felt the first sprinkles of the afternoon, showers that quickly turned into large raindrops. The skies darkened and the wind began to swirl around the clearing. Stepping out once more into the green tunnel of the trail the Bus disappeared behind us as quickly as it appeared out of the wilderness. We were walking again and focusing on the six feet in front of us, only this time we were getting rained on steadily, the sun was hidden behind thunderclouds to the west. The weather that we were certain would remain south of us had turned and was now headed straight for us.

Within minutes of leaving the sanctuary and shelter of the bus, the heavens opened up and dumped. We had layered up our clothes at the bus prior to departure, but the rain and wind cut through easily chilling us to the core. Continuous movement was generating just enough body heat to keep our hands from shaking. At least the downpour broke up the monotony of the trail somewhat. We had spent copious amounts of time trying to keep dry in the early stages of this dumbass trip. Now, giving in to the wilderness and all the water, we accepted we would never dry out and just accepted the fact we would be cold and wet for the next 20 miles back to the car.

Reaching the Tek on the outbound leg, we took a while to dry ourselves after nearly losing Banzai down the river. We dried out, met the hippies, and then bailed off into that frigid waist deep water. Though we were soaked to the bone exiting the river, the sun came out driving the temperature up as well aiding in drying us out. By the time we left the bus we were almost completely dry except for our boots. Dry, wet, cold, dry, wet, cold, wet, dry, wet, dry, sweaty, dry, wet, cold. This downpour started the roller coaster all over again, and motherfucker, it was cold!

The conversations along the trail at this point had deteriorated to resemble delusional ramblings of drunken senior citizens sitting in front of the television at the nursing home with the volume turned down. Banzai was keeping up his relationship with his buddy, Bigfoot. Apparently, Bigfoot had been following us for hours in the woods just off trail. Only Banzai could see him. He was a kind and gentle Bigfoot, like Harry and the Hendersons. He was Banzai's special friend. Smokus was still seeing stop signs randomly around corners, as if paranormal entities from another dimension were trying to persuade him to give in and just end it right there and succumb to the wild. Quitting is easy. Banzai also continued comparing his imaginary playlist in his head with Smokus and me.

Between the ramblings of my schizophrenic friends, the rain pouring down my face and back, and my solid concentration on the next six feet, I had enough to distract me from what I really needed to focus on. Crossing the Teklanika River the first time, the eddies and currents had swirled just right and helped us get to the west bank. As Smokus recalled, the Magic Hippies told us to "hop in here, do a 360 to grab the twig, doggy paddle upstream 2 meters, flop over on your back to grab the grass, pull yourself up on the bank, then cross the second half as fast as you can. Oh, and don't die. Ciao."

Those same eddies that assisted and spit us out on the far bank were going to oppose us on the return trip. We had been up and down that river trying to get to this side, but it never really occurred to me until this point how we would get back. This was my problem to solve and I had roughly four hours to figure it out over the next 10 miles. At least we had water.

The few areas in the road that would have provided a welcome view of the distant mountains were now only gazing areas for gray, hazy rain-covered tundra through the limited visibility. A couple of lakes to the south should have been easily seen under normal circumstances, but with the rain falling in sheets we couldn't even make out the tree line. Up and down the undulating terrain we followed the trail inching closer to the river. Rainwater pooled all along the trail due to improper drainage multiplied by the extreme volume of water falling. If I could find anything about this situation that could bring me back to a "glass half full" mentality, at least the damn mosquitoes were gone. Alaska: home of Mount McKinley, pop-up thunderstorms, and fair-weather mosquitoes. Whatever, I'll take it. I could have also given less than a single shit about bears. At this point, death by mauling would only serve to take me out of my own self-inflicted misery and pay my wife a generous life insurance policy. Love you mama, I did this for you.

In less than 20 hours we were subjected to all types of weather. Cold, hot, sunny, cloudy, wet, dry. My feet were soggy and wrinkled, my face soaked, everything on my back was wet and heavy. Banzai had permanently changed into his sneakers by then. His boots were loosely strapped to his backpack still weighing him down firmly to the trail like anchors. Looking back, he probably brought those boots on purpose just so he could make sure he got a decent workout. Miserable is not the best word to describe our feelings, but its damn close. With each step closer to the river I kept going over my problem in my mind.

How can I ford this river again without ending up in Nenana? I figured the first portion, the wider channel, would not be terribly difficult. The main current in that section was only about three feet wide. We made it across that section easily with the help of our sticks and quite a bit of determination. The smaller braid on the far side would be more formidable. The faster current was certainly not going to help us in any way. My best hope at this point was that the water had retreated slightly with the cooler temperatures of the late evening. Here's a fun fact: hope is not a valid tactic.

Almost every source describing the Stampede Trail, paints a picture of certain doom when facing the Teklanika River, especially during the summer months. The sources mostly all agree that crossing during the summer is a dumb idea and should not be attempted. If hikers choose to test the beast they are advised to try early in the morning when the temps are cool, and the water is lower. The Tek flows from a glacier in Denali National Park, so when the temps drop early in the morning, the river flows less. Makes complete sense. But wait a minute, what about the evening hours? Naturally just due to higher temperatures melting more ice from the glacier, the water flows a bit higher later in the evening. Uh, what about torrential downpours for the last hour or so? Yeah, we're probably fucked.

Stopping to refill water bottles was the only exciting element for this entire phase. We knew we were getting close to the river, but I had given up on checking the GPS. Ignorance truly is bliss. We took a quick break just before reaching the beaver ponds on the west side of the river, refilled our water and noticed the rain had stopped. I guess we had either been so focused or so delusional, we hadn't really realized it before this pause to rest. I honestly don't know how long the rain had been falling, or not falling, for that matter. All I knew was it wasn't falling now. We were certainly no more energetic with this new-found knowledge, so with full bottles, we kept on to the east.

I was in the lead, the rest of the party strung out a hundred yards or so behind me when I heard the distant rumble of the Tek. Tired, emotionally, physically, and mentally spent, I rounded a corner and I was standing on the bank of the Tek. The clouds remained looming overhead, blocking out was left of the late evening sunlight and the air temperature had dropped considerably. The river was in full view in front of me when I noticed a dark blob to the right that didn't seem to belong.

The first channel of the river was maybe 100 feet across. I scanned left and right, up and down stream and saw the outline of something standing just on the western edge of the bank not too far from where I stood. MOOSE!

The Alaska Moose, or Yukon Moose, is the largest of all moose and deer. Bulls can stand seven feet at the shoulder and weigh well over 1000 pounds. Moose appear as clumsy, goofy creatures, but they can certainly be aggressive and protective. If moose are encountered in the wild it is advised to avoid them as much as possible. Though they look docile, they can attack if humans get too close, or if you get between a cow and her calf. My wife actually called in late to work once when we lived in Anchorage because there was a moose laying in our yard next to her car. The hospital she worked at completely understood and told her to come in when able.

The moose to my right was a full grown, slender, golden-brown female. She raised her head from the bush she was so carefully dining on and stared me down, likely due to her 360-degree moose radar. We had a moment. Dumbfounded and surprised, we both just kind of sat there staring, as if to say, "What the fuck are you doing here?" She lost the staring contest when she decided I wasn't worth it and trotted out into the river headed for the east bank. She rushed headlong into the current haphazardly bouncing through the deep water. I wanted to yell "Noooooooooo!" as the entire event unfolded in slow motion like I could somehow save her from certainly drowning in the rushing current, but I realized she was completely making this river her bitch. Effortlessly she stepped across and onto the far shore, scaling the five-foot embankment like a child climbing the ladder at the McDonald's playground slide. Smooth and graceful. I couldn't believe what I just saw. The river that tried to kill my friends, and me has killed people before and will kill people again, was nothing more than a speed bump for this giant mammal. What an asshole!

The moose disappeared into the alder thicket on the east bank, leaving us there to pick up our jaws from the river rock and process what had happened. I think we just stood there for several minutes grasping the situation. She made it look so easy, but we knew we had work ahead of us.

HAIL MARY

You better lose yourself in the music, the moment
You own it, you better never let it go
You only get one shot, do not miss your chance to blow
This opportunity comes once in a lifetime you better
You can do anything you set your mind to, man
—Eminem

A FEW YEARS AGO, my wife and I took an epic RV road trip. Beginning just outside of Boise, Idaho, we made our way east through Yellowstone and Grand Teton National Parks, across Wyoming to Devil's Tower, Mount Rushmore, and eventually into Rocky Mountain National Park in Estes Park, Colorado. From there we traveled west through Colorado and into southern Utah visiting Arches, Canyonlands, Capitol Reef, and Bryce Canyon National Parks, before camping outside Zion. We spent the whole next day in Zion National Park hiking the Narrows, a gorge carved through the landscape by the Virgin River that cuts through the heart of the Park. Hiking was not extremely difficult, but we were walking through the river up to our thighs most of the day. Several miles into the trip we stopped in a side canyon for a quiet lunch break, and began our return back to the bus stop for a ride back to our Jeep.

We reached the bus stop around 1800 that evening and jumped on looking forward to the beautiful scenery as we made our way out of Zion Canyon down the main road of the Park. Along the way, we made a hasty decision to get off and hike as far up Angels Landing as we could, and get back to the bus stop before the last bus came through at 2100. If we missed that bus, we were staying the night in the woods.

Over thousands of years, the Virgin River in southern Utah has eroded and cut through the land that now makes up Zion National Park. The highlight of Zion is the canyon left in the wake of the River cutting deeper and deeper through the local landscape of soft rock. Angel's Landing is a skinny fin of varying types of rock carved by the Virgin River, 1600 feet below the peak. The trail to the top is only about five miles from the trailhead, but hikers must climb a set of 21 switchbacks known as Walters Wiggles just to get to Scout Lookout, a small saddle in the fin a half mile short of the peak.

The final half mile of the hike is risky, to say the least. Hikers must cling to the sides of the sandstone drop-offs like mountain goats. The Park has bolted chains into the cliffs to serve as hand holds to make the climb a little easier but holding onto the chains perches hikers right on the edge of a sheer cliff to the river below. In some places the trail is only a couple feet wide with 1000-foot drop offs on either side. One slip can spell disaster for a hiker.

The Park service recommends hikers with a fear of heights should not attempt to go beyond Scout Lookout, and making the climb during inclement weather is definitely a no-go. The Park Service also recommends four to five hours to complete the round trip, but we only had three hours until the last bus, so we knew we would have to hustle if we were going to make it all the way. We decided to go for it and try to make it as far as we could but leave in time to get down to the bus and back to the Jeep.

The trail starts off easy, but quickly climbs steeply before settling into a flatter canyon. Limited by time we pushed as fast as we could up the slopes and Walter's Wiggles, reaching Scout Lookout at a little before 2000 that evening. After a quick rest and check of the map, we thought we could make it to the end, so we took off down the last half mile. Not even 30 feet into the last portion was the first real steep part requiring chains to traverse. My wife was a trooper and gave it all she had. Surefooted and light on my feet, I was jumping around and flowing over the rocks like a kid playing in the playground at McDonalds. My wife was having a very different experience. She had gotten out on the side of a steep portion and clung solidly to a chain. When a returning hiker told her the trail gets worse just ahead my wife was done. She was completely frozen in fear. She couldn't move either direction. Her eyes shut so tight her face wrinkled. She was stuck. I eased back down to her and took her hand-over-hand back to the Lookout. She had never been that scared.

My wife's hiking day was complete, so she took my backpack, left me with just a small Camelback and proceeded down the mountain, leaving me to finish the last half mile solo. I got to the end, stayed for a few minutes just to take some pictures, then ran the entire way down, back to the trailhead with a couple of college kids from Berkeley, making it just in time to see the bus pull into the parking lot. That picture of her frozen on the side of the cliff is one that I will never forget.

✦

Back at the Tek, dark gray clouds blanketed the sky over the tundra and river. The sun had disappeared long ago, and the air was cold, made colder by the humidity of the rain and the river. The cool breeze chilled our soaking wet clothes. Shivering on the bank with our feet close to the water, but not yet submerged, we knew we were about to be balls deep in the freezing waters of the Teklanika River, once again. Summoning every bit of gusto I could muster I took the plunge first.

The frigid water soaked right through my shoes like a million tiny ice picks stabbing in all directions. As I walked farther out, my legs slowly froze from the bottom up. With every step I got a little closer to the opposite shore, but progress was a tradeoff with the water climbing higher and higher up my lower extremities. Any farther and my tea bag was going to be once more dipped in the ice water. Some people might say, "Just go for it", or "Once you get them wet it gets better." Uh, no, and no, it doesn't. This is a different kind of cold. Like the beaver ponds earlier in the day, this water could make a grown man sing soprano, but this water was flowing and sucking every ounce of radiant heat from my nether regions. It hurt. It sucked. It was also necessary and unavoidable.

I reached the main channel near the far side of the river, the water at my waist right about belt level. Leaning into my hiking stick I stepped across and passed the most dangerous section with just a few short choppy side steps. Smokus was only about 15 feet behind me when I climbed onto the bank and stood on the dry ground of the island. My legs were bright red with frost nip. Helping Smokus up, we looked back expecting to see Banzai following close behind, but he wasn't there. Instead, we spotted him still in the shallows on the other side, like my wife on the fin of Angel's Landing he was frozen with fear and looked slightly panicked. But, but, what the...huh?

The rush of the current beating against the shore was deafening on our side. Banzai was yelling something at us but we legitimately couldn't hear him over the rumble of the river. We had to motion and signal him to come closer, but he hesitated like he couldn't will himself to get in that cold water. He eased closer and closer yelling the whole time. As he got closer to the main channel and we could finally make out what he was yelling, we realized he had broken his hiking stick and couldn't close the loop in his brain on what to do next. His synapses had stopped firing. Sleep deprivation, malnourishment, wet, and cold affect everyone differently. Banzai was in a bad spot. Registering this new information, we convinced him to simply go back and get another stick from the woods. We were in the middle of the forest after all. How hard could it be to find a stick?

Reluctantly, Banzai returned to the other side and exited

the river, disappearing into the woods for a few minutes. I honestly did not think the task was overly complicated. It's not like shopping for a new car. Just grab a fucking stick man. Banzai returned and revealed his choice. Inquisitively he held up his stick to us and asked, "Is this good?" The humor of the situation didn't register until well after the event. Banzai had returned with a forked twig about three feet long and only a half-inch thick. This twig wouldn't hold up my boots over a campfire. It was clear to Smokus and me that Banzai was not right in the head. The miles, cold and wet had taken its toll and wore him down. He couldn't think straight enough to figure out this puzzle. We were of little to no help, either. Freezing cold, but on dry land, Smokus and I were not interested in getting back in that river unless it meant making steps closer to the car. Being cold and wet can make you re-evaluate priorities. This is a chief focus of Navy SEAL training in BUDS. When you've been cold and wet, the last thing you want is to be cold and wet again. Now focus. Solve the problem.

Yelling and signaling some more we convinced Banzai to just wait a minute and we would see what we could do from our side without getting wet again. Smokus and I searched the island up and down for several minutes looking for a suitable and stable pole for Banzai, but all we could find on the 50 by 100-yards wide island was a log about six feet long and six inches wide. Not the best hiking stick by any measure but it would have to do. Best of all, I may not have to get wet again. The only problem we saw with the whole idea was getting it to the person who needed it.

I couldn't exactly hand it to him, and there was no way

I could heave this massive log all the way across the river. Remember, I was NOT getting back in that water. In my daze and deteriorated psychological state of mind, I reckoned I had only one shot at this. Smokus and I motioned for Banzai to get as close to the main channel as he could stand without getting swept downstream. I hiked as far upstream on the island as I could, eyeballed the current and took my aim. Like a Hail Mary pass to end a football game, I chunked that log out into the river with no particular target other than to it get close to the current. The log submerged completely before popping up right in the middle of the channel I'd hoped it would. I watched this entire thing unfold in slow motion. Banzai stood in the middle of a remote river in Alaska, facing upstream, broad side in the current with his hands held out as if to receive a special gift or he was about to get baptized or something. The log meandered its way down stream, spun perpendicular to the current and struck Banzai right in the belt. It could not have been more perfect. Sometimes I guess it's better to be lucky than good. I ain't complaining either way, I'll take it.

Banzai gathered up the log and his wits and made his way to our side of the river. Smokus helped him out of the river and plopped him down on the ground. We all looked ragged and soaked like cats just out of a bath, but we still had one more crossing to go and it was going to be worse than this one.

CHAMPIONS

THE DIFFERENCE BETWEEN a champion and anyone else is an outright refusal to lose or give up when you really want to. Rather than asking "Why did this happen to me?" champions ask "How can I make this work for me?" Sure, talent and skill have a significant impact on one's ability to be a champion. For example, I am six foot three with a decent layer of insulation around my mid-section. I'm probably not what folks look for when shopping for the next champion horse jockey. Even if I really liked riding horses, I just don't fit the mold. Banzai is a short, stocky white dude—probably not a long career in the NBA. Additionally, I may have been super great at ice hockey, but growing up in the south there weren't very many opportunities to play. Sometimes circumstance is a barrier for success. That said, many champions somehow find a way to change that circumstance to fit their goals. Move closer to an area that supports what you want, change eating habits, train harder. These are some ways to change circumstances to your favor.

SERE school taught us about the psychology of being a survivor, and often the difference between success and failure is simply the will to win. Our situation on that island was only going to be changed by one thing. We had to cross the final portion of the Tek. Champions embody mental toughness and resiliency. They have a desire to win and a refusal to lose. Larry Bird said, "I hate to lose more than I like to win." A champion must find a way to endure and continue even when the going gets tough. Sitting there on that island, we were beaten, deflated, exhausted, freezing cold, drained. We needed a win. We had to win. There was no option to lose.

The 10-mile hike from the Bus was my time to try to solve this last obstacle. I tried to block out all the distractions—rain, cold, clouds, Bigfoot, stop signs, imaginary playlists—focus and solve the problem. We sat on the ground, surrounded by brush and alders with the remaining braid of the river only a few yards away and I still didn't have a reasonably solid plan. Maybe I did at one point, but I didn't know what to do from here on. Rather than sit and shiver to death we got up and made our way to the final crossing some 30 yards through the brush. I stared it down intently trying to figure out the best way to do this and not get us all killed.

Nearing the edge of the bank at the same spot we had crossed hours before, I saw the jerky, uncoordinated sway of the small alder breaking up the current. On the previous crossing and relative to the spans of the rushing water, the four-foot square area downstream of the bush offered a gentle resting spot before stepping into the main channel. The way the water swirled on the side closer to us did not offer a suitable path for a return trip. I scouted up and down from where we were standing, but fatigue and cold shivers seemed to cloud my judgment and for the life of me I couldn't see the answer to the problem. I decided to implement the best solution I had thought of during the previous walk in the pouring down rain.

Problem solving is a process. The more times you execute the process the better you get at seeing varying outcomes and selecting appropriate solutions. Military decision-making process, project management process, and observe-orient-decide-act (OODA) loops, are all essentially the same with different words describing the steps. The first step in solving a problem is always to identify the problem. Next, figure as many solutions as you can and select the best one. Finally, implement the solution and see if it works. Military tactical aviators, football coaches, businessmen and parents all use a variation of this process at some point, some more than others. Standing on the edge of that river, I had run as many simulations in my brain as I could think of. Now was the time to reveal my plan to Banzai and Smokus. Our lives may depend on the solution working as it did in my mind.

As I began to describe my finest plan, I removed my back-pack and stripped off a layer of clothes in an attempt to keep as dry as I could. The sun was long gone below the horizon, the clouds were dark and gray, and the slight breeze put a nippy chill in the cold night air. I dug into the depths of my pack to find the item that the entire plan hinged on: the 100 yards of white 1000-pound test parachute cord. My plan was to tie the rope around my waist and wade across the rapids with Banzai and Smokus holding the opposite end tightly in case I slipped. Looking back, I realize this was probably not the best or safest solution we could have come up with, but I was weary from sleep deprivation and my brain wasn't exactly firing on all eight cylinders.

I'm not sure if was an exceptionally good idea or if the other two were just excited I hadn't suggested one of them to be the test bunny. Either way, there was little to no objection from the peanut gallery. I'm positive they were in a similar state of mind and just wanted this episode to be over. I secured my belongings into my backpack and left it sitting next to a small, sapling spruce tree. Trying to pump myself up saying things like "This river isn't going to cross itself", I tied off the rope as best I could to my waist and stepped towards the steep shore.

Banzai wrapped the near end of the rope around the base of the tiny pine sapling. He sat on the ground facing the tree and the river with his foot against the base of the trunk in order to provide a solid anchor for me when I stepped into the current. The bank was steep and a sheer four- or five-foot drop into the fastest portion of the current. The first step was going to be the worst of it and we all knew it. I looked back at Banzai, we exchanged a confirmatory nod that he was ready for the impact and I stepped off the ledge into the river.

The first sensation I remember was the cold. The water temperature felt like it had dropped even more, and I had removed all my layers down to my shorts and a thin, Under Armor t-shirt. That feeling of water stinging my feet and legs was soon overridden by the force of the massive volume and swift current. The depth of the water in this area was up to my belly button and the force hit me like a ton of bricks making the water rise up to my ribs. I felt like I'd been hit by a truck as I lost my footing and started to stumble downstream. I had played this movie over and over in my mind during the preceding hours and it was pretty close to what

I expected. Suddenly and without warning, Banzai gripped the rope as it tightened against the baby tree. The rope jerked taught at my waist and propped my back upright giving me a chance to get my footing and regain my balance. Acting on what seemed like instinct and certainly running on pure adrenaline by then, I stepped carefully across the spans of the water, Banzai letting out inches of rope at a time as I inched forward. Thanks, Banzai. You saved my ass. Reaching for a handful of grass and brush on the far bank I pulled myself out of the water. The worst was over for me, but I wasn't done yet.

The next part was going to be equally difficult. I still had to prepare for the others to cross. We stood on opposing shores just kind of staring at each other like "what do we do now" for a few seconds before I snapped out of it. I removed the rope from my waist and tied it to the base of a substantially bigger spruce tree on my side and yelled for the guys to send me my backpack.

After verifying Banzai had tied of the other end sufficiently, Smokus clipped the pack on the rope with a carabineer and shoved it hard across the water. The rope sagged in the middle, but the pack made it across without incident like an imaginary force was behind it giving it enough energy. I still needed to tighten the rope before Banzai and Smokus could safely use it. Searching around I found a short, broken branch and trimmed it to a one-foot length with my Kabar knife before looping the branch in the rope and twisting as much as I could before I tied each end of the stick to the rope to keep it secure. The rope was taught and ready for Banzai and Smokus to cross.

I recently saw a video on YouTube showing hikers cross the small braid using a small, half-inch thick white rope strung between two trees. The video was dated in July 2009, and clearly showed the area we crossed complete with the small alder bush breaking the current just a few feet downstream. Whether our rope lasted that long is a mystery and I honestly cannot tell for certain. The video posted looks just like the one we installed, but other than a few defining features of the surrounding area, I certainly cannot know for sure. I hope it helped some cross the river, but crossing is always dangerous and clipping into a rope is not recommended.

Banzai and Smokus did what others crossing the river did not. They removed their packs, clipped them to the rope and sent them out ahead of themselves. They also did not clip themselves onto the rope as they stepped into the river; rather, they simply held on for stability and retained the option of letting go to swim for it if needed. The internet is now littered with blogs, stories and videos of successful and unsuccessful attempts to cross the river both with and without ropes. Lucky for us, our remaining party crossed almost effortlessly and climbed out on the east side. Other than being soaking wet we were all good to go. Tired, cold, soaked, but alive, and ten miles from our car.

ZOUNDS!

The better part of valour is discretion; in the which better part I have saved my life. 'Zounds, I am afraid...
—KING HENRY IV, PART 1 BY WILLIAM SHAKESPEARE

SMOKUS AND I departed our houses early one morning in Mountain Home, Idaho, to go hiking in the Boise National Forest just a few miles north of town. It was early June in the high plains desert of central Idaho and the sun was shining brightly making it a great day for some outdoor activity. A bonus was the fact that the wind wasn't blowing with the standard hurricane force it usually does. The drive wouldn't have taken too long but we stopped to splash in a rushing creek for a bit and play with a small rattle snake crossing the road on the west side of Anderson Reservoir. Smokus forbade me from killing it pleading over and over "No, it's nature, it's nature!" I replied emphatically, "Yeah, I know its nature, nature with fangs! If any of my kids end up getting bit by a rattlesnake, I'm taking it out on you!" At any rate, we let the little fella live to see another day, and I spent the next few minutes in the passenger seat arms crossed and pouting. I don't know if the rate of snakebites in Idaho increased or decreased.

All along the road and throughout the forest, the creeks and crevasses were all running at peak capacity due to all the snow melt run off in the adjacent and nearby high mountains. As a card-carrying Oregonian, Smokus drove a thoroughly capable Subaru Impreza, and we used it to wind our way up the narrow mountain road, attempting to get as far up as we could before we hit the snow line at around 7000 feet. The road was rough but passable, albeit a little wet and muddy with all the thin veins of run off crossing as the snow melt sought the path of least resistance to the Reservoir several thousand feet below. Even on hot days in June, such as this, the snow in the higher elevations is still several feet thick, shade covering the slopes and road keeping much of the snowdrifts from completely melting through. I'd even run into snow blocking the roads, exploring this area as late as Independence Day weekend, during past summer expeditions. Reaching one such drift terminated our vehicle travel. So we unloaded the car and set out into the high country on foot, post-holing through snow and mud while still in shorts and t-shirts.

From where we parked the car, we had about three miles and 2000 feet elevation gain to reach the summit of the nearby peak. From there, we could easily look down on either side and enjoy views of several alpine lakes to the north, valleys to the south, and on a clear day we could see all the way to our houses in town. Our path mostly took us north around a series of smaller mountains and rises before we crossed a short saddle and carved out what would make our final push to the top via a series of steep switchbacks. The peaks and slopes in all directions were covered in a veil of white snow and dotted with clumps of black trees, and large outcroppings of rocks and boulders finishing the rugged landscape. The dark ribbon of road cut around the sides marking our path around the bowl beneath the highest peak. Rounding the bend and reaching the midpoint of the saddle we got one of our first glimpses to the south and it wasn't a good sign.

Resting up for what would be our final push to the top we stood for several minutes taking it all in. We'd expected panoramic views in all directions. Instead of unobstructed vistas as far as the eye could see, we could only see a wall of dark thunderstorm clouds and rain pushing from south to north heading right for our location as if we had bullseyes strapped to our chests. The clouds were thick and dark with a healthy helping of cloud-to-ground lightning that was both beautiful and scary at the same time.

We studied the situation for a few minutes and determined the storms were still quiet some distance from us but closing fast, so continuing to the summit was probably not the best idea. After a short Snickers bar break and a handful of pictures, we decided to abort the summit plan and return to the car. If we hustled, we could make it back before the storms got too close and crazy, and we could stay dry.

Heading south to the car and still winding and twisting down the path down the mountain, we now had a clear view of the storms creeping closer to us every second as they rolled across the valley of the Reservoir and up the foothills below us. The sharp crack of lightning and subsequent rumbling thunder echoed through the hills and seemed to surround us in all directions. The sky grew darker as we descended, and the faintest raindrops began to strike our uncovered skin as it was propelled by the windy updraft of the storm climbing the mountain. We knew the worst was yet to come so we hurried along to cover as much ground as we could before things got really bad. We figured if we could at least make it to the denser forest below the tree line we could shelter in place for a while and let the storm pass. Just as we reached a small clearing with a group of spruce and lodge pole pine trees, the storms intensity ratcheted up and we were soon bearing its full wrath. The wind howled and the downpour soaked us. Giant raindrops came from all directions as the wind swirled through the peaks, boulders and trees. The car was still a mile away right in the teeth of the thunderstorm.

We didn't really hesitate at all to get to shelter. In the thinly populated grouping of trees we located a mature spruce tree. The tree was thick and healthy, so much so that it had shielded the ground beneath from the snow and most of the rain. We broke away a few of the smaller boughs around the base of the trunk and slid into the shelter of the tree. Huddling close with the rain mostly blocked in our make-shift shelter, we gathered a pile of small twigs, pine needles and leaves, and a few of the smaller branches of dry dead wood laying around in the mostly dry ground. Using some of the smaller pieces from our cache and a healthy dose of Purell hand sanitizer we started a fire, kept warm and dried out a bit patiently waiting out the storm.

Just as Sir John Falstaff declares in King Henry IV, "The better part of valor is discretion." In other words, taking caution is preferable to rushing headlong into bad decisions. There is a thin line between bravery and stupidity, or insanity and genius. As mentioned before, I try to live my life by a few very simple rules. Rules even the dumb redneck from Alabama can understand and follow. Disciplined decision making and a willingness to recognize and remove emotional bias is fundamental to avoiding bad situations. Whether it's a monetary investment, a choice to get a new puppy, or cross a river in the Alaskan wilderness, these rules and guidelines should be applied. Smokus and I did the right thing on the side of that mountain in Idaho. "Err on the side of caution" is a good motto most of the time. Our hike to the bus was riddled with decision points that could have altered the outcome. Just as I remind my kids when I ask them "Who did this to you?" I was reminded while standing on the east bank of the Tek that we did this to us. We could have certainly armchair quarterbacked our path and pointed out several times where discretion could have or should have been applied. Nevertheless, we were safeish.

Freeing Banzai from the waters of the Teklanika River was a victory for sure—a small one, but a victory just the same. With the three of us safely on the highway side of the river, spent, panting and soaked, I recognized immediately I was in trouble. Up to this moment I had attempted to appear rock solid, focused and determined. I mean, this whole trip was my idea after all, and I was the one the Commander entrusted with the safety of the trip. Remember, I agreed to not bite off more than we could chew. Failing at that command, I suppose I'd be at least a little bit responsible for the deaths of two innocents after the safety board concluded its investigation. I tried to keep my outward appearance of hubris intact, but even the most valiant knight has a chink in his armor.

While Banzai and Smokus were acting like they were tripping on LSD mixed with 'shrooms for the better part of the afternoon, I tried to focus on the task at hand. Left foot, right foot, solve the problem. No sooner than all of us were safely out of the water and back on good-guy land—the correct side of the river—it all came crashing at once and my hands began to shake uncontrollably. I was cold. Very cold. Cold to the bone. In-trouble cold. It was as if I had an epiphany like, "Oh, this is what they meant when they talked about hypothermia." Just like many things, this is something you can't possibly understand until you've felt it. You can read stories and see videos of hypothermia, but they just can't do it justice. Like a blind man seeing flowers for the first time. People may have described flowers to him a thousand times, but until he actually sees them it just doesn't register. I might have been no worse or better off than anyone else, but I immediately recognized the situation. We needed to warm up and we needed to do it fast.

We needed fire and we needed it now. I remember being so cold and shaking so bad I didn't think I could have started a fire, though I so desperately wanted to. I've been cold before. Sleeping outside with my grown-man cuddle buddy in a lean-to just south of Canada in January was cold. Pushing my toolbox out to my F-15 when it was minus 39.8 degrees in Anchorage was cold. "But Roscoe, how did you know it was minus 39.8 degrees? Nobody counts decimal places." Funny you should ask.

Well, the United States Air Force does count decimal places. As of 2004, Air Force Instructions stated the flight line was to be closed when the ambient temperature reached minus 40 degrees Fahrenheit. At minus 39, the assholes at the Maintenance Operations Control Center began to measure decimal places. Work goes on. Oh, and by the way, Air Force, there is no fucking difference between minus 39 and minus 40. Eyelids freeze. Nose hairs and nasal cavities freeze. Everything freezes. Don't be dumb. I digress, a thousand apologies. You get the point.

I have experienced varying degrees of cold many times. I've been every bit as cold in Florida as I was in Alaska, that is until now. Shivering uncontrollably on the River, I was cold to the bone. This is the kind of cold that is debilitating. I couldn't do anything. I was rigidly planted, unable to move except for my violent shivers. Maybe it was the cold water, the lack of sunlight, or just the fact that we were finally across and the adrenaline had worn off, but I was paralyzed. I would have given body parts for a fire or hot bath right now.

After several freezing and shivering minutes, we decided to retreat downstream, past the high ground where we had seen the tent earlier and make it to our previous sitting area and fire ring. With a little luck there would still be a pile of wood lying around and we could begin the process of drying out and warming up. If we could make the quarter-mile trek, we might just be ok.

Bushwhacking down through a thicket of alders and willows and staying as close to the river as we could so we didn't get lost in the woods in the "dark," we noticed a faint glow near the cliff where the hippies had camped. When we finally emerged from the dense brush, we saw the best sight I've ever seen. Standing on the hill surrounded by a dense thicket of black spruce trees were the three Magic Hippies, waving at us and yelling for us to come over. Behind them was a blazing campfire!

MAGIC HIPPIES:
PART DEUX

ONE OF THE final scenes in the 2013 film Captain Phillips starring Tom Hanks is powerful. It depicts the Captain, a rock-solid figure throughout an emotionally intense, pressure cooker style situation of hostage and power struggle. Captain Phillips maintains composure and focus for the entirety of the ordeal, but once safe with the situation resolved, he breaks down. All that pent-up emotion burst loose like a dam breaking and releasing a flood. I have never felt that kind of emotional suspense at that level, but I came damn close standing on the edge of the woods looking up the hill at three young, plaid-flannel-wearing hippies inviting us to their fire. I don't know if they will ever know exactly what it meant to us at that time, but they quite possibly saved our lives.

We managed to struggle and stumble our way up the escarpment to the campsite, and although weary, wet and ragged, we dropped our bags and collapsed beside the campfire. The relief from the cold was instantaneous, but we each had a long way to go before being completely comfortable, dry and warm. Systematically over the next few minutes, we stripped down and replaced our wet clothes, socks and shoes with as many dryish garments as we could. Each of us gathered a few sticks from the healthy pile of firewood the hippies had gathered and shaped them down to usable supports to suspend our wet clothes and shoes close to the fire to assist them in drying. After only a few more minutes of work to get comfortable we were able to relax a bit by the fire.

In addition to being a basic tool for ultimate survival—preparing food and forging tools and weapons—fire is known to be hypnotic and arguably therapeutic for the mind. Several books and articles in various outdoor and science publications have covered the history of fire and its impact on civilization, but a few stretched farther, noting the remedial, social and psychological effects fire can have. In short, fire relaxes humans and takes them to a near-meditative state, allowing the brain to unwind and relax. The portion of the brain activated during meditation interweaves with the portion governing "working memory," a critical element allowing the brain to focus on more than one thing at a time and relate them to each other. Additionally, a simple fire is a reason for people to congregate socially. Sitting around a fire, solving tomorrow's problems while remembering today's experiences makes for great conversation and mental stimulation. Fire is good for the mind, body, and soul.

To this day, I still look forward to taking my family camping, sitting around a fire and not saying a word. We just stare at what we've always referred to as "campfire TV" and relax a while. My son and I sat next to fire for what may have been a couple of hours one time when we were out by ourselves. Not a word was spoken. Just before I cashed in and retired to the tent to get ready for bed, I looked at him and said, "Good job, bud." He looked puzzled and replied, "Why, what did I do?" I simply replied, "Nothing, and that's the point. Way to not screw it up."

Sitting by the hippy fire we were finally relaxed and warming up a little more every minute. Our three Magic Hippies had spent the day reading their bibles, contemplating the meaning of life, and most importantly staying high and dry. The six of us sat around staring into the orange flames as the fire crackled and popped from the dry spruce and pine wood, telling stories and replaying the last few hours out loud.

The hippies informed us that we had mentioned what time we left our car and what time we arrived at the Tek earlier in the day—our initial introduction that interrupted our cigars and oatmeal. Using that information, they thoughtfully deduced our relative pace and rate of travel, applied that to the distance to the bus, plus about an hour for relaxing at the bus, prior to returning, and adding in the 10 miles from the bus back to the river. They completed their algebraic algorithm with a little slop for the weather and river crossing, recognized the sun would be down and we would be freezing cold from crossing the frigid water in the dark.

Putting all this together like renowned theoretical astrophysicist Brian Green scribbling furiously at the chalkboard, they had the situation and time down to plus or minus an hour, built a fire and waited. I can imagine them basking in the sun that afternoon watching the storms roll in, chewing on a straw of grass contemplating the calculus. Take 10 miles, add a bus, figure in a brief dialogue with a German stranger, add thunder and rain plus 10 more miles, carry the 2, divide by the square root of cold to the three hikers and wet rushing river, but multiply by a factor of tired and delirious. Clearly when you do all the math, it equals midnight-thirty Sunday morning. For three young, scruffy nomads they sure had this crap figured out and they were spot on. They humbly said, "We figured y'all would be back about this time and you would be cold." Good hippies, good.

I honestly can't remember the conversation, but I do remember laughing about how dumb we were to try the hike to the bus in the manner we did. I guess hindsight truly is 20/20. We all propped up our wet clothes and gear as close to the fire as we could to try to dry them out. Banzai found the exact distance from a fire where a pair of black Asics GT-1600 running shoes will melt. He managed to snatch them away from the fire before they were a total loss, but not before the campsite was filled with the stench of melting nylon and rubber. Even with the smell of burning rubber, and sweaty, drying clothes all around, this was the first time in a long time we all smiled and laughed.

After socializing for a while, maybe an hour or two, the hippies turned in for the evening (morning) and retreated to the warmth of their tent. Banzai, Smokus and I, brandishing dry clothes for the first time in many, many hours, bedded down as well. Smokus was the only intelligent one of us (I told you he was wicked smart). A few days prior to departing the base, he stopped over at the Base Exchange and bought a cheap sleeping bag. Brilliant! Since this was supposed to be "survival school" style, and the fact that I didn't want the added bulk and weight, I had packed only a thin foil space blanket. Banzai was the worst off bringing a cheap, thin blanket from his hotel room wrapped in a plastic shopping bag. It was one of those poly-something, slippery, inefficient piece of shit blankets that only ends up on the floor by the end of the night because it won't grip anything, so nobody uses them. Flimsy and porous with the consistency of cheap plastic, it holds little to no warmth and isn't even that comfortable. Smokus was snug as a bug, and I contemplated beating him with a stick and taking his sleeping bag. I was ok until the fire went out, but Banzai tossed and fussed with that damn blanket the entire time.

I think I managed to get a short nap, but when the fire went out around 0400 with no one to feed it, I got up and got dressed, followed shortly by Banzai, fed up with his tussle with the blanket. He looked like he'd been getting his ass whipped in a UFC fight all night. We had to wake Smokus out of a warm slumber, so we could get back on the trail and cover the remaining 10 miles back to the car. Trying to be as quiet as we could to not wake up our three saviors in their tent, we departed the campsite just after 0400 Sunday morning, made our way down the path to the north and into the riverbed.

The sight at the Tek in the early dawn hours was surreal. Masked in shadows and faint, pale sunlight, the landscape was still slowly coming to life, not quite changed from shades of gray to the first rudimentary colors as the sun was still too low on the horizon to really make them pop. Steam rose from the water even as it raged northward toward the narrow canyon, and the roar broke up the quiet peace and tranquility of the surrounding forest. I stood there, wearing every stitch of clothing I brought with me, shivering as I took my last looks at the formidable river. The worst part of this moment was not that I was cold and shaky, but that I knew just 200 yards down the trail we would be once more stomping in knee deep icy water. After soaking to the bone in the glacial runoff and subsequently drying out completely by the fire, the last thing any of us wanted was to get wet again. Discouraging, yes, but at least this time we were heading towards home. We turned east and started the final push, leaving the Teklanika River behind us for the last time.

The next ten miles were not remarkable in any way other than they were quiet and laborious. Our conversation had withered into a few short, curt questions regarding our ability to remain on the trail and how much farther we had remaining. The only two recounted stops per our video records were the Savage River and the mud flats. We made the Savage at 0600 Sunday morning, full daylight and sunshine warming us, surrounded by brush for the first time in two hours since departing the Tek into the green tunnel of the trail. Standing on the bank after crossing the Savage, we added up our elapsed time to this point to "48 hours based on a 0600 wake up Friday morning." 48 hours with a little fitful sleep and very few calories. We had walked for 30 miles, crossed two rivers twice, and were running low on energy and lucidity.

FINISH STRONG

THE REMAINING MILEAGE to the car was a grind, to say the least. Left foot, right foot, left foot, right foot. Everything hurt. My feet were swollen, my legs weak and heavy, vomit on the sweater, mom's spaghetti. The three of us stumbled and staggered our way back to the car only wasting the energy to speak when completely necessary. Arriving at the car just before 1000, we threw our bags in the back and sank into the seats. Finally finished walking and looking forward to completing the final leg of the trip, Banzai closes his video diary: "Hour, like 40, we just made it. As you can see, we're all here, barely. I can't believe we did it. But we did, so now we're gonna go into our work call. Anyway, it's been real, it's been fun, hasn't been real fun. Peace."

Smokus jumped in the driver's seat, I climbed in the passenger side and Banzai was asleep before his head hit the bench seat in the rear. Only two things were on our minds at this point: get food and get home. Our plan had limited our timeline to between 30 and 32 hours for the hiking portion of the trip. We arrived at the car just over 31 hours after departing. #Nailedit!

Pulling out of the clearing we had parked in 31 hours before, Smokus turned us east down the paved portion of Stampede Road. I was drifting in and out of consciousness when I heard the crunchy scrape down my side of the car. Smokus had drifted off to never-never land as well and started to run off the road. He and I knew now this adventure was far from over. We were still over three hours from home.

We spent the next eight miles talking to each other just to stay awake. Reaching the intersection of the Stampede Trial and Parks Highway, we decided to head south initially into the town of Healy to try to find some food. Sorry, Banzai, you chose sleep over a vote in the process. We pulled into the first place we saw on the left, a lodge with a restaurant in the front. The only problem we had with the plan to replenish our calorie deficit was the damn restaurant was closed. It was 1000 Sunday morning and all we wanted was a cheeseburger!

After waiting a few short minutes in the parking lot, the place opened, and we were able to get our burgers. The best cheeseburger I ever had. Honestly, it was a crappy cheap burger, but I would have put mustard on a car tire and eaten it at this point on my road to complete malnourishment. Bellies full, caffeine digesting, and ready for the final push, we loaded up once more in the same configuration. Banzai repeated his trick of falling asleep as he sat down in the back seat. Smokus pulled us out onto the highway and headed north. Finally, after what we would later recall as a life-changing experience, we were sitting with full stomachs and heading back toward Fairbanks and the Air Force Base. It didn't take long for all that to come crashing down into reality.

I tried as hard as I could to stay awake and help focus Smokus on the road in order to avoid certain death. If we'd hiked all that way and died in a car crash on the way home, what in the world would people think of us? We hadn't made it but just a couple miles when without warning Smokus pulled over into the grass past the shoulder and off the pavement, almost into the ditch. He looked at me and just said, "Dude, I can't do this." I told him "Don't worry, man, I got this". We played a half-version of Chinese red light and swapped seats after running around the car. I sat down, buckled my seat belt and grabbed the steering wheel. Immediately I knew there was no way I could make it all the way, so I looked at Smokus and just said, "Nope." I never even put the car in gear.

With the engine still running on the side of the Parks Highway two miles north of Healy, we slept like babies for about an hour. I woke up and felt like a million bucks. Rested and determined, and still on the clock for our work call, I drove the rest of the way back to Eielson AFB. The drive was unremarkable, and I'm pretty sure Banzai slept the entire way.

We pulled into the lodging building on base somewhere around 1400 Sunday afternoon. With two hours to spare until we had to be in for mission planning, we parted ways and disappeared into our individual rooms. After ditching my backpack and shoes, I stripped down and sank into a hot bath for over an hour. I could have slept for days, but I managed to gather my wits and get to work. The hardest part was putting on my boots because me feet were so swollen and sore.

The work call was uneventful, but by God, we made it. Fellow squadron members who knew we were going out to the bus asked if we made it or not. When we answered yes, there was no applause or champagne, no hype, no nothing. Much like our unceremonious arrival at The Bus just hours prior, people seemed legitimately indifferent to the result. Of course, they had no idea what really went into completing the trip, and we were way too tired to tell the story. They had no idea how far we'd walked, how cold we were, how wet, how hungry. They knew nothing of mud and hippies and rain and mosquitoes. They just kind of shrugged and went about their business. I didn't care in the least. All I knew was my feet hurt.

TRAGEDY

WHILE THE BUS remained more than 20 miles down the Stampede Trail in its original location for many years, it was, and likely still is, surrounded by a cloud of controversy. Area locals argued and lobbied for years to have the bus removed due to the annual visitors constantly requiring assistance. In other words, they were tired of rescuing so-called "pilgrims" who get in a tough spot due to unpreparedness fueled by fanaticism. Many Alaska natives completely scoff the idea of the bus being a quasi-holy place for the McCandless faithful. Rather, they argue it would just be another back country shelter were it not for one person's overzealous pride, audacity and gross under-estimation of the Alaskan wilderness. Either way, people from all over the world continued to attempt the hike, many succeeding and some failing.

Hikers should know the Stampede Trail is primitive and non-existent is places, so thorough planning and consideration is paramount. Alaska is still wild, and the trail is not maintained. This specific area of Alaska is not necessarily "remote" by Alaskan standards, but should not be taken lightly. The bus location was less than 30 miles from the Parks highway, a major north-south thoroughfare through the Alaskan interior. Just six miles south of the bus site is a Forest Service outpost cabin, and there are a few private cabins scattered out in a small radius. Lastly, Denali National Park is less than twenty miles south, but while the Denali Road is decently trafficked, this area near the park is off the beaten path.

Since Sean Penn's full motion picture "Into the Wild" based on Krakauer's book was released in 2007, there have been two documented deaths on the Teklanika River. A Swiss woman and a Belarusian woman drowned crossing the river, both losing their footing and getting swept downstream. Local Sheriffs and State Troopers have noted there have been countless rescue attempts along the Stampede Trail, as well. The movie, maybe more than the book, sensationalized the bus, putting it on a pedestal as some sort of shrine for McCandless disciples. Just like in 1992 when McCandless spent four months at the bus, Alaska is still wild. Hikers heading down the Stampede Trail in search of Fairbanks Bus 142 (or its former location) should be alert and prepared when setting out, and they must know and understand the dangers along the way. Regardless of how you feel about this story, it is always sad to hear about death or otherwise avoidable tragedy.

So why did I highlight these tragedies? For a few reasons. First, these deaths were the results of what seem like terrible, yet simple, mistakes. Mistakes anyone could make. Mistakes we made or came very close. I've been just as guilty as either of these two young ladies in terms of taking risks or trying hazardous methods I had not tested. Maybe we were just lucky, but it doesn't take a rocket surgeon to recognize how the outcome of our hike could have been drastically different had any one of our decisions panned out slightly differently.

Second, the dangers of adventure in the wilderness should be brought up for conversation. Communication is key. Share experiences. This is no time to play the "keep a secret" game. I love the idea of learning from others' mistakes. The information available via the internet seems to be never ending, and I promise you are probably not the first person to face whatever particular problem or obstacle is in your way. Without casting judgement and pointing fingers to assign blame, we should all take a look at the lessons learned and try to apply them in the event we may be faced with similar challenges.

Lastly, this could have very easily been us on our trip. Unprepared and full of zeal and possibly a little ego, we could have been swept away just like either of these young women, and ended up as a statistic. Many of the rules and laws governing the safe conduct of society are "written in blood." We very well could have added more blood to the pile. Thankfully, our trip ended happily. Tragically, many do not. Everyday people head out for fun and meet disaster. Preparedness and experience can help prevent death or serious injury. Always take the time to properly plan, brief and execute within your known limitations and capabilities, and you won't end up a statistic.

The internet is full of naysayers declaring openly how stupid and reckless folks are for attempting a hike like this. I disagree. The hike itself is not difficult. Honestly, it's just long. To be completely fair, with the proper planning and choosing the proper time of year, this hike would be stupid easy and be over before you know it. Other than being long and boring at times, it's not an overly difficult trail. There isn't a significant number of major obstacles or elevation gain, and if you do it at the right time of year the weather can be fabulous. The only real threat to a seasoned outdoorsman or experienced hiker is a river crossing, and even that would be a piece of cake, if executed properly with the correct gear.

Still, people braving trails just like this one get into trouble every year. Everyone should take precaution and go with knowledge and proper gear. The internet is filled with lists and videos providing gear options for any adventure, including river crossings. Take a blow-up raft to ford the river if you must, but don't complain to me when you finish the 40-mile round trip and say, "That was boring and dumb, why did I just do that?"

THE END OF AN ERA

AFTER MANY YEARS of reminiscing this story with family and friends, my wife convinced me to finally put it down on paper. I can't remember how many times I've told this story, or portions of it, to captive audiences and unwilling listeners alike. Each time I tell it, I say aloud if not just to myself, "Man I wish the other two were here to tell you this from their own perspectives", and "That was a great trip." With each telling I laugh almost as hard as I did the day it happened at some of the downright foolish decisions and thought processes we had that long weekend in 2009. Any one of those decisions would have altered the story in some way. As it turned out, our trip could never be recreated, and I think it played out exactly how it was supposed to.

I received an email from an old friend on June 19, 2020. The email contained a link to a news article and the simple sentence, "The end of an era." Over the next couple of days, I received several texts and emails from family and friends with the same or similar links embedded. The news story first sent to me was from CNN, and was titled "Alaska's 'Into the Wild' Bus, known as a deadly tourist lure, has been removed by air".

The article goes on to describe how the Alaska Department of Natural Resources, along with local authorities, decided to move the bus out of public concern. On June 18, 2020, a CH-47 Chinook helicopter from the Alaska Nation Guard airlifted the Fairbanks 142 bus from its resting place along to the Sushana River to an "undisclosed location." With so many recsues and deaths over the years, officials deemed the bus and the route to get there too much of a hazard for hikers. Despite creating an exact replicate mockup of the Bus in the town of Healy, visitors still braved the elements and wilderness in hopes of a photo op next to the famed Magic Bus.

In July 2020, the Department of Natural Resources entered in negotiations with the University of Alaska's Museum of the North to be a final resting place for the bus. The historical and cultural significance of the bus could not be understated, and all parties agreed it should be preserved so the public could enjoy it in a safe manner. As of September 2020, the bus had arrived on a long flatbed trailer at the Museum where it likely will rest in peace forever.

When it was moved, the Bus was in disrepair. Over the years, "pilgrims" have abused and looted the Bus, shot bullets holes into it, stolen items, and disgraced it. Looking at pictures of the Bus today compared to when we were there 11 years ago, it doesn't even really compare. When we were there, the mattress still had fabric on it. The paint wasn't nearly as worn. Much of the glass was still intact. It seemed that in 2009 people legitimately still respected the memorial aspect of the Bus. Of course, nothing lasts forever, and the more people visited the Bus, the more people destroyed it, inch by inch.

The museum intends to attempt to maintain the originality

of the bus, while at the same time ensuring safety for the public in all aspects. Designs are being brainstormed for how the final display will present, and Museum officials are referencing and consulting with many people to ensure authenticity. Chris McCandless' sister, Carine, was quoted by the Museum after giving her inputs. According to Alaska Public Media,

> "She says it can be a powerful educational tool, including about the mistakes her brother made that led to his starvation in the wilderness.
> "He wasn't prepared. And I don't want people to gloss over that fact," she said.
> The Museum is predicting at least two years of fund-raising required to complete the exhibit.

We made our trip in 2009. Eleven years later, almost to the day, the Bus is gone. I mentioned before a couple of times that our trip could not be recreated. Now, with the bus removed, that realization is a certainty. Now there is no real reason for anyone to brave the cold water, peat bogs, mud flats, beaver ponds, two rivers, rain, sun, thunderstorms, hyperthermia, calorie deficiency and sore feet. Like I said, it's not even a tremendously pretty place to go. There are much better hiking destinations within just a few miles if someone wanted a truly tantalizing experience. If I were to go out four-wheeling, maybe it would be a cool trail to go down. As for hiking, I could do without.

The only thing that motivated us and kept us going was the Bus at the end. I hope moving the Bus prevents any future mishaps along the Stampede Trail. I am also grateful I got to experience the journey while it was still in good shape.

CLOSING TIME

"Don't cry because it's over. Smile because it happened."
—Dr. Seuss

IN THE FALL of 2018, I was the head football coach for the West Valley Spartans 13U eleven-man tackle football team in Surprise, Arizona. We finished our season undefeated, 9-0, and won the State Championship, but the story began in April when I and a couple of other coaches were on the fence about joining a different club. We finalized our decision and began preparations for the upcoming season. We recruited over the spring and summer, had coaches' meetings and player camps and began to build the blueprint for how we envisioned our season turning out. When we finally started practice in August, we had only six weeks until our first game.

Approaching our first game, my confidence in the team was low. We only had six returning players, and 17 players who either hadn't played football at all, had not played tackle football, or hadn't played for me in my system. I would have sworn to you we were going to finish the season 4-4, maybe make the playoffs and probably lose the first round.

We continued to work hard every week to learn and hone our craft. We put in the time and hard work to get better every time we strapped it on. Three times we came from behind to win. It wasn't always pretty, but we moved on to the next challenge and kept our eyes on our goals. By the time we played the Championship game it was anti-climactic. Almost like we knew we would win because we had put in the work. I remarked to the coaching staff at how thorough planning and preparation had made coaching the game really boring, almost as if we knew the outcome before the first whistle. We took pride in the win, but I told the team afterwards we didn't win the championship on that night. We won it in August and September when we worked our asses off to be the best team we could be. We never gave up. We never accepted our status quo or defeat.

Words cannot describe the pride I had for our team and our coaches. Everyone from QB1 to the tee holder to the water boy found their role and executed it at a high level to achieve the overall goal. The best part was in that moment right after the game, I addressed the team and presented them with the five-foot trophy they earned. I asked them if anyone cared about or remembered the up-downs, push-ups, hitting drills, sprints, or heat. A resounding and thunderous "NO SIR!" was the only answer. Nobody cared about the pain at that point. It was 100% worth every ounce of sweat and every hour of practice. We made a goal, and we did whatever it took to complete that goal. We were Champions.

Another example of forgetting the pain and torment of

never quitting happened on a random Saturday while temporarily assigned in Las Vegas. I once hiked Mount Charleston, the mountain with the eighth highest topographic prominence in the United States, with a terrible hangover from hanging out at Buffalo Wild Wings drinking beer all day watching college football the day prior. I thought I was going to die. When I got to the top and had my Gatorade and granola bar, I forgot all about the pain on the way up. All I cared about was soaking up the sun and enjoying the magnificent view from 11,918 feet above Las Vegas, Nevada.

Yes, I know 11,918 is the elevation above mean sea level, and Las Vegas sits at roughly 2000 feet elevation. So technically, the view from Mount Charleston is roughly 9918 feet above Las Vegas, Nevada, give or take a few inches, I'm sure. Thanks for pointing out that mathematical error.

Looking back on our Bus trip, I get similar feelings as that Mount Charleston climb. I remember how bad it was at times, but the experience cannot be duplicated. The stories we tell about that hike bring memories back that only the three of us have. I don't feel the cold in my bones, the swelling in my feet, or the hunger anymore. I remember those feelings clearly, but I don't think I would have it any other way. I'm glad we did it. Anything worth having is worth working hard for.

Our hike into the Alaskan bush is not unique or special in any way other than it was ours and it makes us laugh to this day. Many people traveled to the Bus (or attempted) each year, and they did it for various reasons. Some are "disciples" of Chris McCandless' anti-establishment philosophy. Others, like Hendrick, just wanted to see what all the fuss was about. And still, a few like we just want to get out into the wilderness for a while and reach a destination. The point was that we had a goal and we reached it.

There was nothing spectacular in the area that would lure people down the mucky, wet and soggy mosquito infested trail other than that broken-down shell of an old transit bus. No stellar view off a mountain peak, no honey hole fishing spot, no gold mines. Just tundra and forest and a bus. Trust me, its anticlimactic.

Still, predicting and planning for every aspect of a journey into the bush can be challenging due to the constantly changing weather, geography and water. The conditions of any of these can change without notice. Remember my previous comment about driving five minutes out of town, taking a left and getting lost in the wilderness.

I will admit there is something to the idea that Alexander Supertramp lived life on his own terms right up until he decided to return to civilization. Maybe we all can relate in our own way. I've never wanted to be the kind of sheep that falls in line, necessarily. I also don't want to go too far out of my way to buck the system or step on my own dick. I guess my point of view is, leave me alone and I'll leave you alone. Maybe there's something about keeping your shit to yourself. Maybe there's something to being alone and not relying on anyone except you.

I can appreciate the idea the young man had when he ditched his worldly belongings for a simpler life without bounds, but that is no substitute or validation for being unprepared. No doubt it was a hard life at times, but I'm sure he felt solace, confidence and freedom. Ironically, Mother Nature stepped in and sealed his fate one way or another, taking his choice away and making him live life according to a certain set of rules. I suppose we are all dependent on something after all.

Also, don't let negative people establish your goals for you. Anything worth having is worth working hard for. Do the time, plan it out, train for it and enjoy the ride. Alabama Head Football Coach Nick Saban says, "Mediocre people don't like high achievers, and high achievers don't like mediocre people." Be confident and positive in your preparation so the journey is easy and enjoyable. Alternatively, don't hate on those who have dreams and the drive to turn those dreams into goals, and then see them through to reality.

I guess I'd regret if I didn't address the Magic Hippies and the role they played in this saga. I have told this story many times, and I've let a handful of people read the very rough drafts of this book. Everyone that hears or reads this says the same thing, "You know those hippies were angels, right?" My immediate response is always, "Or, they were devils."

Think about it, if we had never met the Hippies on that beach, we would have retreated to the safety and security of our car, returned to Fairbanks and the Air Force Base, and never put ourselves in harm's way in the first place. The simple addition of those three characters changed the outcome and story forever. Was it a chance encounter? Was it divine intervention? We will never know. I am positive that without the Hippies we would have never attempted to ford the river again and continue onward to the Bus. I am equally positive that without them we may not have survived the aftermath on the return trip.

The lesson I take away is simple enough. Be mindful of the people you choose to surround yourself with and take advice from. They may have good intentions, but those intentions could lead you down a difficult and dangerous path without careful consideration. Though they may seem like they have your best interest in mind, you still need to remain objective and make sound decisions with the new information.

In our case, we could have internalized the Hippies knowledge of the river crossing, filed it away, and still chose to return to our car. We knew when we crossed the river, we were in it for the long haul, but we did not know exactly what the trip would require from that point. We leaned into our emotions and made a subjective decision rather than remaining objective. We should have taken the new information and objectively quantified and qualified it to make a rational decision. Instead, we reacted based on excitement and jubilation and set our course.

You should always try your best to remain objective and leave emotion out of the decision-making process. We failed to do that and almost got caught in an unsolvable problem. Thankfully it all worked out and we have an awesome story to tell, but the lessons remain.

My wife has a sign in our house that reads, "My favorite thing is to go somewhere I've never been." Although it was probably mass produced, and likely the brainchild of some soccer mom on the crapper who got rich selling dumb sayings printed with her Cricut on cheap balsa wood for those of us who have nothing better to do, it characterizes my family's sense of adventure. Road trips, four-wheeling, hiking, glamping, it doesn't matter. Pack a backpack and get out there. See the world. Hike the hill. Walk down the dirt road. Throw rocks in the river. For the love of God, don't drink the water!

I still don't have expensive gear or ultra-light equipment. I am not the type of guy to spend multiple hundreds of dollars to lower my overall weight by a couple of ounces. I still get out and enjoy the outdoors. Solo, with family or with friends, it doesn't matter. Just get off the couch and go for it. You'll never know what you are capable of it you don't try.

Recently I listened to the audio version of the book "Can't Hurt Me" by David Goggins. Goggins is a retired Navy SEAL who holds many distinctions, is a world-class ultra-runner, and has a great message about the power of mental toughness and fortitude. One lesson from his book hit me hard. He told a story about a dream or inner thought that he had. In this dream, he was an old, 300-pound, retired roach exterminator standing in line waiting to meet God after his time on earth was done. He was third or fourth back in line and began to take note of what was happening in the front of the line.

Each person that stepped up to meet God was met with a chart of his or her life. God went over the chart in detail and either approved or disapproved. When Goggins stepped up he and saw his chart. The chart had the following listed: punk kid that was called racial slurs, beat mercilessly by father, cheated through school, failed the Armed Services Vocational Aptitude Battery (ASVAB) 3 times before finally meeting minimum requirements, lost 106 pounds in 3 months to become eligible to become a Navy SEAL, went through three "Hell Weeks" in SEAL training before finally passing, ran 101 miles in under 24 hours with no training, broke and set the Guiness Book of World Records for pull ups by doing over 4000 in 24 hours, set course records as an ultra-runner, and many more.

Goggins, fat and old, smelling of roaches and filth looked at God and said "That's not my life, you got it wrong." God smiled back at him and said, "No Goggins, this is the life you were supposed to have."

This resonated with me. I don't want to be the one on my deathbed with regrets. I want to be the cool dude at the nursing home telling hell-raising stories making all the other geriatrics jealous. I want my kids and grandkids to want to be like me. I want them to wish they had the adventures I did. I want to try it all. I want to do it all. I don't want to lie there in the end and have God show me what my life was supposed to be. I'd rather him have to keep a watchful eye on just what the hell I'm going do next so he can update the list. Just like I told my football players, I am going to leave it all on the field.

That said, at the rate I'm going I probably will not make it to the nursing home. Instead, I'll die in some fiery crash going Mach 10, or fall off a cliff, or some other ridiculous accident while enjoying another adventure. At least I'll go out with a smile on my face and adrenaline in my veins.

PARTING SHOTS

WINNING BEGINS WITH mindset. You have to develop skills and techniques, for sure, but if you do not have winning mindset, you will never reach your full potential. Below are a few of my keys to winning at any task. Whether you are going for a promotion at work, tying your shoes in the morning, or heading out for a backcountry adventure, follow these steps to be a champion.

Keep choppin' wood. Sometimes life is a grind, and you have to just slog it out. Nobody likes choppin' wood, but if you chop long enough, you'll look over and see a nice big wood pile and be proud.

Don't Suck. Anything worth doing requires maximum effort. Work hard and do the best you can at everything, and you will get what you want in the end. If you try every day to not suck, or at least suck less, then you are improving and getting closer to your goal.

Move the Ball. Championships are won and lost sometimes by merely inches. Every play and every down, the offense's goal is to move the ball. If you consistently move the ball in the football game of life, you'll get first downs, first downs lead to touch downs, and touchdowns win games.

Create your own luck. If luck is the combination of preparation and timing, you are 100% in control. Work hard, make good decisions and be persistent. Create opportunity. Always give 100%.

Compete hard. You can always compete with yourself. Compare yourself to the person you were yesterday, set goals for tomorrow, and measure your actions daily. You'll be surprised at what you can accomplish when you focus on what matters and keep going.

Improve. Make a little progress every day. Learn from your mistakes, plan and achieve. Aggressively seek and destroy anything that prevents you from reaching your goals.

Never quit. Silence your inner quitter and keep going. The road is long, and each step gets you a little farther. Keep moving.

Win. It's not enough to say, "I want." Finish that sentence with "And this is what I'm prepared to do to get there." You do not need to be the most talented or smartest person. Be patient. Eventually doors will open, presenting opportunity.

Be a champion. Nothing can stop a relentless competitor willing to outwork everyone else. Preparation, hard work, and timing create opportunity. When opportunities arise, be confident and seize them.

Lastly, plan, get out, and explore, but know there are no new lessons, just lessons re-learned.

*"Life should not be a journey to the grave with the
intention of arriving safely in a pretty and well preserved body, but rather to skid in broadside in a
cloud of smoke, thoroughly used up, totally worn out,
and loudly proclaiming "Wow! What a Ride!"*
—HARRY S. THOMPSON

*And on the 8th day, God created backpacks, hiking
shoes and water bottles, and He said, "Get out
there and enjoy it dummy, I made it for you!"*
—ROSCOE

ACKNOWLEDGEMENTS

Sitting here trying to remember every person who had an impact or influence on the adventure of bringing this book to completion seems like a task comparable to the hike itself, daunting and near impossible. As I look back through the many memories and characters, I find it hard to give some credit while possibly leaving others out. I am not sure I account for everyone or everything that played a part in bringing this book to completion, but here goes.

I absolutely could not have done this without the love and support of my wife, Katie. I am the first to admit that I married up. She is a bright light that shines like a beacon for me to keep going in the right direction. Sometimes her support comes in the form of just looking the other way, and I am sure this was 100% the case for this adventure. She, like many others, had no idea what was really going on when I told her we were trying to get to the Bus. She only knew I would be out of cell phone range for a few days, and hopefully she would receive call Sunday night from me telling her we were safe. I thank you for never holding me back, encouraging me to be adventurous, and allowing me to follow my arrow wherever it points.

I would have never had this memory or completed this book without Banzai and Smokus. We three will always have a bond connecting us wherever the universe takes us. The next adventure is already in the planning phase as I write this. Thank you both for the encouragement and inputs. Lace 'em up tight boys.

As this book neared completion, I got in touch with Joel Hughes through a mutual friend. Joel guided me through the journey of finishing and publishing like a champion. He is always positive, even if I am having a bad day. His warm spirit kept me at ease as he coached me through the end phase of getting this book out to the reader, no easy task. Thank you, Joel, for your counsel.

After a few years of writing, editing and re-writing, I had a rough draft that I thought was good enough to share with some trusted friends and family. I sent this book out to a handful of people, maybe a baker's dozen, but only six read it in its entirety and gave me good, constructive feedback. Katie White, Donna Johnson, Jana White, Jim Burnette, Enrique Garcia, and Jeff "Curly" Wills, thank you very much. I may call on you again for another project!

For all the family and friends over the last 13 or so years who afforded me the chance to tell the story, whether it was the 5-minute version, or the full blown 12-pack version, thank you. You didn't realize it at the time, but you were encouraging me and helping me remember the flow and details of the story. Also, a big thank you to the few who sent me emails with attached news articles about the Bus and the goings on in the area. I have them all saved and I valued that more than you know. Thanks to all.

Lastly, I would like to thank anyone who reads this. Of all the things I thought I would be when I grew up, an author was never one of them. Thank you for taking the time to read my story. I hope you enjoyed it and can take some lessons away without having to subject yourself to what we went through. Remember there are No New Lessons, just lessons re-learned. Thank you.

Below is a small excerpt from my next book, WORK HARD DON'T SUCK coming Spring 2023.

COMING SOON:

WORK HARD DON'T SUCK

A COUPLE OF YEARS before mom and I got married, I got a chocolate Labrador Retriever, Sarah Jane Rottendog. Sarah and Tyler immediately became best friends because they were both "onlys". Tyler was an only child until he was six years old when Niki was born, and Sarah Jane was an only dog until Ozzy the cat. Yes, Ozzy and Sarah were best buddies, and I'm pretty sure Ozzy thought he was a dog, but I digress. Sarah was well trained and loved to play fetch with whomever or whatever. She and Tyler had a special game they would play.

We lived in a small, two-bedroom house on Elmendorf Air Force Base in Anchorage, Alaska. We would take Sarah for walks when we could, but due to the weather there was much time spent indoors so Tyler and Sarah played together a lot. Tyler would get one of Sarah's toys and take her down a couple of small steps next to the front door. He would command her to sit and stay and she happily complied. She would sit there for several minutes not moving a muscle except to cock her head occasionally to make sure she could still figure out where Tyler was. Tyler would hide the toy somewhere in the house and return to Sarah, still sitting tall with ears perked ready to pounce.

Tyler would stand in front of her, cross his arms and just stare at her for a while. After several moments, Tyler would finally yell, "Go get it!" Sarah took off like a bolt of lightning with her nose glued to the floor trying to find her hidden treasure. After a thorough search she would find her prize and return to Tyler who was still standing near the front door. This game went on for hours. She absolutely loved all you boys.

Sarah was our greeting party when we brought Niki home from the hospital in 2002, and Caleb in 2004. We sat both of you down on our couch in your car seat bucket thingy, and Sarah licked and loved all over you. She adored all of you from the moment she met you. All of you at times would lay in the floor with her, pulling her ears and jowls. She just smiled and played along. That dog loved her babies. She had no idea if you would grow up to be knuckleheads or gentlemen. She didn't care.

Every day I come home from work, and I am met with our trio: Tucker, Jax and The Dude. They have no idea whether I had a good day or not. They are oblivious to my mood. All they know is that I am home, and they are happy. Most days, Jax will follow me into my room, wait until I change clothes, then low crawl across the floor for a good booty scratch before we go join the rest of the family in the living room. He just loves. It doesn't matter what I've done that day.

Sammy loved on mom like no other dog I've known. I've

never seen a dog dote on a person like Sammy doted on mom. He was special for sure, and he loved unconditionally. Regardless of what kind of day mom was having, Sammy was always happy to be with her and showed it through his affection.

Be the person your dog thinks you are. Your dog doesn't care if you are tired, irritated, hungry, agitated, need a shower or otherwise had a bad day. Your dog always thinks you are the best thing in the world. Your dog thinks you hung the moon. Your dog thinks you are the most awesome human on the planet. When you think about the simple statement "Be the person your dog thinks you are", you recognize you have a lot to live up to.

Living up to the standard your dog has set can be challenging. Maybe dogs are put here to remind us about things like "don't sweat the small stuff" and "be happy". I don't think I've ever come home and found my dog in a bad mood telling me off because he's just grumpy. Dogs think you are the best. Try hard to live up to that standard. Take the lessons contained in this project and apply them. You may find that the simple changes and aspirations get you closer to being the person your dog thinks you are, a high bar for sure.

DO ORDINARY THINGS EXTRAORDINARILY WELL

Since moving to the greater Phoenix area in 2016, our family has not missed many opportunities to take advantage of the vast array of extracurriculars scattered throughout the Valley. From concerts to football games, hockey games to NASCAR races, plays and comedy shows, Phoenix always has something to go see and experience. One event we have taken advantage of each year is the annual Red and White Scrimmage of the Arizona Cardinals NFL football team.

Each August, the team invites the public to a free practice viewing and scrimmage inside State Farm Stadium in Glendale, Arizona. Getting to go to an NFL game is always cool, but I always find it interesting to get a chance to see a little behind the scenes. You know, to get to see how the sausage is really made. Arriving early assures us decent seats down close to the action for sure, but it also allows us to take in the entire experience from stretching and warming up to the full-on scrimmage.

As a football coach and a fighter pilot instructor, I enjoy seeing the details in this event. Every year I've gone to the Scrimmage I have remarked about the same thing: the Arizona Cardinals do the same drills we coached at the youngest youth levels and all through high school.

I sit back in my seat in awe as I watch the receivers precisely running routes and practicing catch-tuck-run drills. Linebackers always do the lateral shuffle bag drill and practice proper form tackling. Offensive linemen practice exact placement of their feet and hands. Quarterbacks practice throwing with proper mechanics. The athletes and coaches on the field have been in the sport for decades and are at the top of their game. They are literally the best at what they do for a profession, yet they still practice the fundamentals.

This tells me a lot about what it takes to reach the pinnacle of whatever you have set for your goal. You are required to do the ordinary things extraordinarily well to rise above the competition. If you never take the time to master the small details, you will never be able to achieve the big goals to their fullest. The athletes on the field for that scrimmage practice the same, ordinary boring drills they have practiced since childhood. If they do not enforce the fundamentals, they will inevitably make mistakes and begin their downward spiral ultimately yielding their position to someone who works hard at the basics.

This is true in any profession. I had a conversation not too long ago with a fellow instructor pilot about a young student on an upgrade flight here at Luke Air Force Base. The four-ship of F-35s had flown out to the Sells Military Operating Area and fought against another flight of jets. Make no mistake, switching from tactical flying to administrative flying is always difficult, but its fundamental to what we do every day. If you can't do the administrative phases great, you'll never be good at the complicated tactical portion of the flight. The student in question apparently had a good flight up to the return-to-base phase, where he either could not or would not get in position and fly a good formation up to the base. Flying fighters requires precision placement of your aircraft and a zeroed focus on the task. There isn't a lot of room for mistakes when you are flying literally inches away from another jet going 350 knots. The student failed his upgrade ride because he was not able to do the ordinary things extraordinarily well.

You boys are getting set to venture out into the real world and begin what is hopefully a long and prosperous career and family life. If you do not pay attention to the little things and master the mundane, you will never achieve the highest you can reach. Paying attention to the little stuff must become a habit. Do the ordinary things extraordinarily well. Be extraordinary.

APPENDIX

SINCE McCANDLESS' MISFORTUNE in the area, many hikers have dared the rapids of the Tek. Several times over the years, rescue crews have been summoned to the Tek to retrieve those in peril. More than once over the years, death has been the ultimate price paid for attempting to reach the Bus. A young lady named Claire Ackerman died in 2010 while attempting a crossing, over a year after the time we crossed and strung a rope across that small braid. Like our crossing, she tied herself into a rope strung across the River leaving her no escape or exit strategy should something go wrong. As she stepped out into the current, the force took her feet out from under her and she fell in. The rope sagged into the water with her still attached and prevented her from gathering herself and getting up. Kaylin Bettinger authored an article in the Anchorage Daily News dated August 16, 2010. The excerpt reported the following:

> "A Swiss woman who drowned Saturday was trying to ford the Teklanika River less than a mile from the famous bus where Chris McCandless died almost two decades ago.

"On Saturday, Claire Ackermann, 29, from Switzerland, was backpacking the Stampede Trail in Denali National Park and Preserve with a partner from France, whose name has not been released but who was about the same age, said Alaska State Trooper Eric Jeffords. They attempted to ford the Teklanika River, just north of Healy. The famous bus was just on the other side of the river, though Jane's partner told troopers that is not where they were heading.

"Here's what Jeffords was told happened before he got to the scene: The pair had met traveling, and they had been in Alaska about two months. They were about 13 miles into their trip but were unfamiliar with the terrain.

"Jeffords estimated they tried to ford the river around 4 p.m. To help brace themselves against the fast-moving water, each tied one end of a rope around their waists. They then tied their rope to another rope strung between two trees on opposite sides of the river. But that rope had too much slack.

"The river was running high, and Jane and her partner were swept off their feet. Ackermann was unable to regain her footing. The rope between the two trees drooped into the water, keeping her rope under as well. She was stuck underwater.

"Her partner was eventually able to cut his rope and let the river carry him to the bank. He then ran back up the bank, waded into the river and cut Jane's rope. The two were then swept about 300 yards downstream of the trail. Ackermann's partner attempted to give her CPR but was unsuccessful."

The following are news articles about the two known deaths. The first recorded death, other than McCandless, was Claire Ackermann noted in the previous article. The second and most recent death was in June 2019. A young Belarusian woman died while attempting to cross the Teklanika River using a rope not unlike the first young woman.

From the Los Angeles Times:

'INTO THE WILD' FAN DIES TRYING TO REACH MCCANDLESS' BUS

August 17, 2010 | 4:05 pm

Jon Krakauer's 1996 book "Into the Wild" told the story of Christopher McCandless, an idealistic young man driven to leave his comfortable bourgeois life behind; traveling through increasingly unpopulated areas, he sought a kind of truth, a closeness to nature. Eventually, he wound up in Alaska, where he camped out, deep in the woods, in an abandoned Fairbanks city bus. Trapped by a swollen river too turbulent for him to cross, McCandless eventually died in the bus, probably of starvation.

On Saturday, Claire Jane Ackermann, a 29-year-old from Switzerland, died trying to reach the bus while crossing that same river, Alaska State Troopers report. The AP reports:

Troopers say 29-year-old Claire Jane Ackermann attempted to cross the Teklanika River with a 27-year-old man from France on Saturday when they lost their footing and were pulled under by the current, according to the Fairbanks Daily News-Miner. The man survived.

The old Fairbanks city bus was where 24-year-old Chris

McCandless camped out and starved to death in 1992. It has become a destination for adventurers.

McCandless' story was made into the 2007 film "Into the Wild" starring Emile Hirsch, directed by Sean Penn. The film, which racked up a stack of nominations and awards, helped popularize McCandless' story.

Krakauer's book opens with the story of Christopher—who was calling himself Alex—getting a ride out to the Alaska backcountry. "Alex pulled out his crude map and pointed to a dashed red line that intersected the road near the coal-mining town of Healy. It represented a route called the Stampede Trail. Seldom traveled, it isn't even marked on most road maps of Alaska. On Alex's map, nevertheless, the broken line meandered west from the Parks Highway for 40 miles, or so, before petering out in the middle of a trackless wilderness north of Mt. McKinley." Krakauer probably never imagined that other unfortunate travelers might use this description as a map of their own.

—Carolyn Kellogg

Husband recalls trying to save his wife in fast-moving river during trip to 'Into The Wild' bus

Christopher McCandless starved to death in 1992 in this bus on Stampede Road near Healy, Alaska. (Jillian Rogers/AP)

By Morgan Krakow
Staff writer on the General Assignment desk
July 27, 2019

A Belarusan woman died trying to cross a fast-moving river in Alaska during a trip to see an abandoned bus made famous by the book and movie "Into the Wild."

At close to midnight on Thursday, Piotr Markielau, 24, called the Alaska State Troopers to tell them his wife, Veranika Nikanava, 24, had been dragged underwater in the Teklanika River, just outside of Denali National Park. The two had married in New York less than a month earlier.

After spending two nights at the bus, the couple had run low on food and decided to cross back, Markielau told The Washington Post. By 6 p.m., they had reached the river and the water was higher than when they crossed days earlier. Markielau traversed the river first and said his legs were tired by the end.

About two-fifths of the way across, Nikanava called out for help, Markielau recalled. He waded into the water, and then his wife lost her footing. She hung on to him as he attempted to drag her to shore.

"I felt really horrible at that moment," Markielau said.

About 75 to 100 feet downriver, he was able to pull her to land, and he said he believes she died in his arms.

He left her body by the river and walked four hours before he was able to find other people and called authorities.

"She was really loving," Markielau said. "She was the most kind person I've ever met. She was really sharing this love with everyone. I got the bigger part of this love."

On Monday, authorities confirmed they are investigating the incident, but did not suspect foul play.

The water was rapid and waist-high, said Ken Marsh, a spokesman for the Alaska State Troopers. The segment the couple tried to cross was higher because of recent rainfall.

Situated along the Stampede Trail, the abandoned Fairbanks City Transit Bus 142 has become somewhat of a pilgrimage spot in recent decades, sometimes with a devastating ending. The trail is more than 100 miles southwest of Fairbanks.

Christopher McCandless, who hitchhiked to Alaska after graduating college, and donating his life savings, lived in what he called the "Magic Bus" for about four months. The story of his travels, and his death within the bus in 1992, was captured in a book by Jon Krakauer in 1996 and later in a 2007 film directed by Sean Penn.

Since then, the bus has drawn curious visitors to its rugged site.

Some hikers come to the bus because of deep emotional feelings they have toward McCandless and his story.

"I spoke to people who said they felt like the bus was a sacred place," said Eva Holland, who has written about "Into the Wild" pilgrimages. "They felt like it had a special kind of magical aura about it."

Others, such as a group of hikers whom Holland profiled, are just curious about the site.

Locals' sentiments about McCandless and the pilgrimages

he inspired, vary. Some feel quite negatively about him, that he approached a journey in an unforgiving area of Alaska and was not prepared for its hardships. Others are more understanding.

From Outside Online Magazine, July 2019:

EVA HOLLAND

Jul 29, 2019

24-year-old Belarusian woman died while attempting to reach the abandoned bus made famous by Christopher McCandless and *Into the Wild*.

Veranika Nikanava and her husband, 24-year-old Piotr Markielau, were crossing Alaska's Teklanika River, just outside Denali National Park, when Nikanava lost her footing and was swept away. Markielau made it to shore and was able to retrieve his wife's body downstream. He contacted the Alaska State Troopers just before midnight on July 25, and was retrieved by a police officer and volunteer firefighters on ATVs. According to Ken Marsh, a spokesman for the troopers, the couple had been married for less than a month.

The river is the primary obstacle in the popular but dangerous hike to the bus. It's fast and cold and can run waist-high or worse in high water. Sometimes there's a rope strung across it, intended to help hikers. But that doesn't guarantee safety: Nikanava reportedly lost her grip on the rope when she fell. In 2010, another young hiker, Claire Ackermann of Switzerland, drowned in the Teklanika under similar circumstances.

The bus sits 20 miles down the Stampede Trail, and roughly ten miles past the river crossing. A longtime shelter for hunters passing by in the fall, in the summer of 1992 it was home to Chris McCandless for several months. McCandless had been roaming and adventuring across North America for a couple of years before he wound up on the outskirts of Denali, where he hoped to survive off the land. He crossed the river and found his way to the bus in April, with winter still holding on. Later that summer, hungry and hoping to retreat, he found his way back blocked by the river at high water. He died in the bus in late August and was found by moose hunters in September.

His story was first told in a classic *Outside* feature by Jon Krakauer, "Death of an Innocent." Krakauer published a book-length version, *Into the Wild*, in 1996, and soon after that, a trickle of pilgrims, inspired by McCandless' idealism and commitment to living life on his own terms, began making their way to the bus. The trickle increased after the film adaptation of *Into the Wild* was released in 2007, and by the time I found my way to the Stampede Trail in 2013 to write a story on the "McCandless pilgrims" phenomenon, locals estimated that a couple hundred hikers were seeking the "Magic Bus" each year.

On that trip, the chief of the local fire department told me he'd already rescued a dozen pilgrims during that summer season alone. When I hiked to the river to see it for myself, I watched three hikers get swept downstream by the current. (They survived with minor injuries.) I heard rumors that locals planned to blow up the abandoned hulk in order to solve the problem; a few years later, a local newspaper columnist wrote that he'd always figured "two cans of gas and a match" offered a similar solution.

This second death will likely renew the conversation about whether or not to remove or destroy the bus. But it's just as likely, given the remote location and the costs involved, that nothing will change this time, either. Twenty-seven years after McCandless' death, his story continues to capture the imaginations of young people—many of them, now, not even born yet when he died. It's hard to squelch that kind of emotion.

In a statement, the Alaska State Troopers urged travelers to "come prepared" for Alaska's wilderness, and its "challenging weather, water, and geographical conditions." That's good advice. My own advice? Find another hike, another trail—there are plenty of them. There are better ways to honor an adventurer you admired than by following a dangerously well-worn path.

DO YOU WANT TO BE A CHAMPION?
DO YOU WANT TO LEARN HOW TO CONSISTENTLY WIN AT LIFE?

Visit https://1of5project.com to learn what it takes to win in every area of your life.

The 1 of 5 Project's Mission Statement:

IMPROVE. IGNITE. INSPIRE.

The 1 of 5 Project's mission is to Improve your personal standard, Ignite change with a champion's mindset, and Inspire others through your own actions.

https://1of5project.com

Regardless of your starting point, **The 1 of 5** Project will guide you to better decision-making, mental discipline, and physical well-being to improve your own standard and increase everyone's average.

The 1 of 5 Project applies proven techniques from intense experiences as a championship winning coach and combat aviation veteran to serve clients with problem solving, goal setting, planning and performance. Start with yourself. Change the world.

At **The 1 of 5**, we specialize in providing life coaching services via books, coaching, public speaking engagements, emails and more.

Visit https://1of5project.com to learn more.

9798987002001